W9-DAT-273

The Jesus Road

Kiowas, Christianity, and Indian Hymns

by Luke Eric Lassiter, Clyde Ellis, and Ralph Kotay

University of Nebraska Press : Lincoln and London

Portions of chapter 2 and the afterword were previously published as " 'From Here On, I Will Be Praying to You': Indian
Churches, Kiowa Hymns, and Native American Christianity in
Southwestern Oklahoma," *Ethnomusicology* 45 (2001): 338–52,
published by the University of Illinois Press.

Library of Congress Cataloging-in-Publication Data
Lassiter, Luke E.
The Jesus road : Kiowas, Christianity, and Indian
hymns / Luke Eric Lassiter, Clyde Ellis, and Ralph Kotay.
p. cm.   Includes bibliographical references and index.
ISBN 0-8032-2944-5 (cloth: alkaline paper) –
ISBN 0-8032-8005-x (paperpack : alkaline paper)
1. Kiowa Indians–Religion. 2. Christianity–Oklaho-
ma. 3. Hymns, Kiowa. I. Ellis, Clyde, 1958- II. Kotay,
Ralph. III. Title.
E99.K5 L35 2002 264'.23'0899749–dc21 2001043059

FOR MILDRED KOTAY (1926–1999)

In whose loving memory all royalties will be donated to her former

church, Cedar Creek United Methodist Church, Carnegie, Oklahoma.

Contents

Illustrations

Acknowledgments

Many, many people helped us bring this book to life. First and foremost, we would like to thank those in the Kiowa community who so graciously gave their time and energy to make this work possible. In particular, the members of Ralph's Kiowa hymn class had a special role; over the many years that Ralph has taught this class, they have continued to encourage him to talk about hymns, their meanings, and their future. For this, Ralph is especially grateful.

Several people worked with us directly on forming many of the ideas that we set forth in this book. When this project was in its earliest stage —that is, when Clyde and Eric embarked on a project on the Saddle Mountain Kiowa Indian Baptist Church—Vincent and Grace Bointy, Cornelius Spottedhorse, and the late Cy Hall Zotigh were instrumental in helping Clyde and Eric understand the role of Christianity in the Kiowa community. Mary Aitson, Helene Fletcher, Margaret O'Pry, and Dean and Bell Reeder offered further insights on Saddle Mountain the place and Isabel Crawford the missionary. Thanks also to Herbert Westner, who allowed all three of us to visit the Saddle Mountain Church in Cache, Oklahoma, where it has stood since he moved it there more than three decades ago. In many ways, this visit changed the direction of Clyde and Eric's Saddle Mountain project to encompass a larger story posed within its current collaborative framework.

After completing the first draft of this manuscript, Bessie Ahaity, Anita Blackbear, Vincent Bointy, Robert Cannon, Frances Doyebi,

Donna Kotay, Milton Noel, Pat Kopepasah, Robert Pinezaddleby, and Doris Poolaw reviewed it closely and offered a number of helpful comments. Our deepest thanks to Theresa Carter, who made an extra effort —as she so often does—to get the manuscript out to those Kiowa people who were interested in what we had to say about Kiowa Christianity and Indian hymns. We would also have to include here Danieala Vickers—Theresa's daughter—who did much to encourage this project early on, and the families of Emily Satepauhoodle, Shirley Tanedooah and the late Billy Gene Williams, Billy Evans and Dorita Horse, Jessie and the late Harry Tofpi, Jennie and Ron Bemo, James and Dru Ponkilla, Jimmie Lee and Clifford Blanchard, Edith Harjo, Delo Kahrahrah, and Chuck and Pawnee Duncan—who often and regularly housed and fed Eric and Clyde on their many trips to Oklahoma. Their support and generosity helped make this book a reality.

We would certainly be remiss without acknowledging the singers whose voices help make up the accompanying compact disc. Once again, our thanks to Ralph's Kiowa hymn class, whose diverse voices extracted from several years of class recordings constitute a good bit of this CD. Thanks also to Pat Kopepasah and Letha Peters for their willingness to re-record, with Ralph, several songs in late December 2000.

Ball State University (especially the Department of Anthropology and Provost Warren Vander Hill) and Elon University (especially the Department of History, Dean Nancy Midgette, and Provost Gerald Francis) provided the means for the three of us to gather on both campuses in the fall of 2000 and conclude this collaborative effort. Finally, we would like to thank our families for their patience, reassurance, and guidance. With this in mind, we have dedicated this work to Ralph's late wife, Mildred, who inspired us all to recognize the Spirit of God in each and every person.

Introduction

by Luke Eric Lassiter

In mid-June 1998, Ralph Kotay, Clyde Ellis, and I drove to Cache, Oklahoma, to meet Herbert Westner and to speak with him about the Saddle Mountain Kiowa Indian Baptist Church. Westner, a local businessman, purchased the church and its outbuildings in 1963 and subsequently moved them from Saddle Mountain to his amusement park in Cache. Although we did not know it at the time, our visit to the church—the first ever for Clyde and me, and the first in decades for Ralph—would prove to be a turning point in our work with one another and with the Kiowa community. For as we sat in the church and listened to Ralph and Westner exchange stories, our initial plan for a history and ethnography of the Saddle Mountain Indian Baptist Church gave way to a larger discussion of Christianity and Kiowa history.

The Baptist missionary Isabel Crawford established the Saddle Mountain Mission in 1896. Led by its headstrong missionary and a devoted congregation, Saddle Mountain was flourishing by the turn of the twentieth century, when it dedicated a fine new sanctuary building. In 1903 and 1904, however, Crawford and the congregation were rocked by harsh criticism when the Saddle Mountain deacons appointed Lucius Aitsan, a Kiowa, to serve communion. Because only white, male, ordained ministers could serve communion, the church's decision—which Crawford openly and vocally supported—led to so serious a breach with the American Baptist Home Mission Society that the church was formally reprimanded, and Crawford was forced out in 1906. Deeply embittered, she remained unrepentant and forgot neither the controversy nor the Kiowas. Through letters, conversations, and published accounts, Crawford never let the mission society forget either. And the Saddle Mountain Kiowas never forgot her. When she died in 1961 in Canada, the congregation sent for her body and had her buried in the church cemetery.[1]

Interestingly, shortly after her death—when the congregation had dwindled to just a few members—the Mission Society sold the church and its land to a white family, the Reeders, who were local farmers. With the Kiowa congregation now officially disbanded, the Reeders were concerned about the church falling into disrepair, and they contacted Herbert Westner, an avid collector of historic buildings, to see if he was interested in moving and refurbishing it.[2]

"[They] wanted to know if there was something we could do to save that church," Westner said to Ralph, Clyde, and me. "So we moved it." Westner moved the Saddle Mountain church eleven miles south to his amusement park, Eagle Park, where he had assembled a collection of historic buildings, including Quanah Parker's famous Star House. Westner said that almost immediately various local congregations asked permission to use the church on Sunday mornings. Years later, even after Eagle Park had closed, people continued to gather there. "While the people were using it," Westner said, "we tried to maintain [the church] the best we could."[3]

After some discussion, Westner asked Clyde, Ralph, and me if we wanted to see it. Indeed we did. Ralph had attended Saddle Mountain as a boy with his parents, and although he had seen the building during visits to Eagle Park, he had not seen the interior since he was a child.

Ralph, Clyde, and I jumped into Clyde's station wagon, and we met Westner at the locked gates of the old amusement park a mile or so away. There, directly opposite the gate at the far end of a spacious compound, stood the church. Westner unlocked the gates, and we entered the grounds. Walking past an old trading post, buildings from the original Fort Sill, and Quanah Parker's Star House, we approached the church's steps.

Ralph was silent as Westner unlocked the church doors, but as we walked into the front hallway, Ralph inhaled a deep, long breath and turned to Clyde and me. "It's just as I remember it," he said in a slow whisper. "It's just as I remember it."

He reached out to touch the wall as he made his way into the main sanctuary. Stained glass windows refracted a dim glow into the small, quiet space. A few birds chirped outside as Ralph made his way over to one of the wooden pews. "It's just as I remember it," he said again. Ralph reached out to touch the pew's back. He moved his hand across the wood as if he was remembering an old friend.

Ralph looked toward the front of the sanctuary, looked back at us, and turned his attention toward the front again. "I can just *see* my mother standing there," he said, reminiscing. "I can just see her." Ralph paused. "This is where Mom and Dad would sing their Kiowa hymns, right here."

Christianity and Kiowa Hymns
The Story of a Collaborative Project

In many ways, this collaborative project began on that summer day when Ralph, Clyde, and I visited Herbert Westner and the Saddle Mountain Indian Baptist Church. Clyde Ellis and the University of Nebraska Press had just republished Isabel Crawford's 1915 memoir *Kiowa: The History of a Blanket Indian Mission* as *Kiowa: A Woman Missionary in Indian Territory*. Soon after its publication, many Kiowa people expressed great enthusiasm and interest in the book. Both Clyde and I consequently found ourselves engaged in several conversations with Kiowa people about Saddle Mountain in particular and Kiowa Christianity in general.[4] In fact, Ralph, Clyde, and I interviewed Westner to

1. Clyde Ellis (*background*) looks on as
Herbert Westner (*left*) and Ralph Kotay
(*right*) talk inside the old Saddle Mountain Kiowa Indian Baptist Church where
it stands today in Cache, Oklahoma.
Photo: Luke Eric Lassiter, 1998.

address the questions prompted by our own conversations about the events leading up to the relocation of the Saddle Mountain Church to Cache.

After our visit with Westner, Clyde's historical interest in schools and missions, my ethnographic interest in Kiowa song, and Ralph's lifelong personal experience with and dedication to Kiowa Christianity and hymns began to come together in an interesting way. Ralph and I had worked closely together on Kiowa hymns for a chapter in my first book, *The Power of Kiowa Song*.[5] In the process, I learned that much more could be said about Christianity in the Kiowa community. But because the book primarily concerned powwow songs (especially Kiowa Gourd Dance songs), Ralph and I talked about the possibility of doing a separate project on Kiowa hymns one day, but it really had not taken shape. The publication of *Kiowa: A Woman Missionary in Indian Territory* began to change that, however. Clyde's work for the introduction to Crawford's memoir coupled with his research on Kiowa schools in *To Change Them Forever* had also prompted him to think more deeply about the role and meaning of Indian churches in the Kiowa community. Our conversations with each other and with Ralph that summer day persuaded all three of us that a book on the Kiowa Christian experience was badly needed. Indeed, much of the American Indian studies literature lacks serious attention to Christian experience in general; scholars more often than not choose either to dismiss it altogether or pose it as mere assimilation into the American mainstream.[6]

Ralph, Clyde, and I consequently began to talk about a new book project. At first, the natural course seemed to be a coauthored project on Isabel Crawford and Saddle Mountain by Clyde and me, a project that Ralph agreed to closely advise. For the next year, Ralph introduced us to several church people around Saddle Mountain, helped us with interviews, and remained intimately involved in our ongoing conversations about Christianity in the Kiowa community.

As Clyde and I worked together on the history of the Saddle Mountain mission, however, several things became increasingly clear. First and foremost, Christianity in the Kiowa community was and is much more complex than the Saddle Mountain Indian Baptist Church; although the story about Isabel Crawford and the church is compelling, it points to a much larger story.[7] That larger story, of course, includes the experience of Kiowa Christians like Ralph. But as Ralph and so many other Kiowa people repeatedly expressed, the singing of Kiowa hymns is central to that experience. To be sure, a book on Kiowa Christianity without hymns would be like a church without a minister. As so many Kiowas say about these hymns, "These songs minister to us."

Clyde and I came to this conclusion, of course, primarily because of our ongoing relationship with Ralph. Ralph regularly reminded us of how important Kiowa hymns are to his own life in particular and to the Kiowa Christian tradition in general. Indeed, like many hymn singers in the Kiowa community, Ralph has dedicated much of his later adult life to the preservation of Kiowa hymns precisely because the unique Kiowa expression of Christianity *itself* is threatened (see part 2). With this in mind, Ralph began teaching a Kiowa hymn class in 1993, and he has recorded countless songs for future Kiowa generations.[8]

Thus, in the summer of 2000—two years after our meeting with Herbert Westner—Ralph, Clyde, and I decided that the best way to approach a book about both church history and Kiowa hymns would be to take into account our different approaches and perspectives. Such a project would necessarily combine Clyde's history, my anthropology, and Ralph's personal experience.

This book, then, is an attempt to do just that. Split into two parts, part 1 is written by Clyde and frames the broader encounter with Christianity in the Kiowa, Comanche, and Apache community. As a historian, Clyde combines sociopolitical history, ethnohistory, and ethnography to suggest Christianity's changing role over time. Importantly, Clyde sets forth both the events and causes surrounding its adoption. With this historical context as our backdrop, Ralph and I in part 2 explore the experience and meaning of Kiowa hymns. In particular, as an anthropologist I combine ethnography and ethnomusicology to impart how language in speech and song has brought about a unique Christian practice that situates Indian churches specifically within the Indian community of southwestern Oklahoma. Ralph, as a Kiowa, combines his personal experience and his song preservation work to discuss more specifically the Kiowa hymns on the accompanying compact disc (a discussion that Ralph and I together compiled and edited). Here, Ralph's words ground the entire manuscript in Kiowa song; he makes all the more clear just how important it is that scholars reconsider Native American Christian experience. More importantly, however, Ralph clarifies the higher purpose for this book: to preserve the knowledge surrounding Kiowa hymns. That knowledge, as will become apparent, includes both hymns *and* the Christian heritage that gave rise to these songs. Thus, although we approach the topic from different perspectives, Ralph, Clyde, and I are each making a similar point. As Clyde writes in part 1, "There is no doubt that for a great many Kiowas, Christianity is a fundamental part of their culture and world."

The Kiowas: A Short History

The Kiowas first migrated onto the plains from present-day Montana. According to oral tradition, an argument between two rival chiefs led one chief and his band to migrate northwest and the other, with a larger group, to cross the Yellowstone River and move to the northern plains around 1700. There, these Kiowas (and the Kiowa-Apaches, who were a small, linguistically unrelated group who were allied with the Kiowas well before their historical period) lived in close proximity to other established groups, and their relationship with the Crows, Arikaras, Mandans, and Hidatsas led to a rapid adoption of the Plains lifestyle.[9]

During their early tenure on the northern plains, the Kiowas occu-

2. Ralph Kotay (*left*) and Luke Eric
Lassiter (*right*) prepare part 2 of
the manuscript at Ralph's home.
Photo: Robert Dean Kotay, 2000.

pied the Black Hills while maintaining their alliance with the Crows. Near the beginning of the eighteenth century, however, the Lakotas and Cheyennes began exerting pressure on them from the east and northeast. As a result, the Kiowas moved southward until they encountered the Comanches, with whom they warred for control of the southern plains until the close of the century.[10]

Like the Kiowas, the Comanches also migrated onto the plains around 1700. They entered the region from the Rocky Mountains and shared a linguistic and social affinity with the Shoshones to the northwest (in and around present-day Wyoming). Their close association with the Shoshones was supposedly broken because of misunderstandings between the two groups. As with the Kiowas, the Comanches probably first moved onto the southern plains due to pressures from other groups (e.g., Blackfeet and Crows) to the northeast and the desire for a more abundant supply of horses in the Southwest—an important element for the growing bison-centered economy. The Comanches were among the first of the Plains Indian groups to acquire horses, and as mounted warriors, they dominated much of the southern plains.[11]

The Comanches and Kiowas fought for control of the southern plains until the late eighteenth century. According to tribal accounts, hostilities between them ended around 1790 when two groups of Kiowa and Comanche warriors unknowingly visited the home of a Spaniard with whom both parties were on friendly terms. Upon hearing about the presence of their sworn enemies, the Kiowa and Comanche contingents prepared to fight one another, but their host intervened and encouraged them to establish peace. The men then met and discussed the prospect. One of the Kiowa men and a Comanche captive who lived with the Kiowa agreed to remain with the Comanches until the fall season to negotiate an accord. If they did not return, the remaining Kiowa warriors would avenge their deaths. They did in fact return, and the following fall the Comanches and Kiowas gathered again at the home of their Spanish host and peacefully put to rest years of conflict.[12]

Allied with the Comanches, the Kiowas became one of the most formidable powers on the southern plains. They were at war with other powerful nations such as the southern Cheyennes and Arapahos until the mid–nineteenth century. By forming alliances with such groups as the Mescalero Apaches and the Wichitas, the Kiowas were able to increase their range markedly, even raiding as far south as northern Mexico.[13]

In general, the Kiowas shared with other groups on the plains a number of sociocultural institutions: a nomadic lifestyle, a bison-centered subsistence, a focus on warfare and military societies and their exploits, and an emphasis on individualism. The acquisition of horses, in particular, defined this Plains lifestyle. And the Kiowas, like the Comanches and many other Plains peoples, were well known for their massive herds. As was true for many Plains people, the accumulation of horses through trade or by raiding neighboring groups became one of the foremost activities of the Kiowas. But horses embodied much more than their obvious function. They carried enormous symbolic and practical capital; prestigious warriors and their families increased their status and power by the number of horses they owned.[14]

As mounted warriors, the Kiowas were both wealthy and powerful. They staunchly defended their territory, and through much of the first half of the nineteenth century they presented a fearful obstacle for Americans who traveled through the southern plains on their way to California or the Pacific Northwest. For these Americans the southern plains were desolate and worthless, and their chief concern was safe passage through the region.[15]

American interests in the region began to change, however, when the U.S. government established Indian Territory (present-day Oklahoma) in 1834 for the forced resettlement of eastern tribes. This removal policy initiated several conflicts with the Kiowas over territorial claims and served only to escalate hostilities between the Kiowas and Texas settlers, who refused to recognize Kiowa territorial claims. Around the same time cattle and farming interests began to grow in the region as well, and as agricultural activity grew, violence on the southern plains increased many times over.[16]

By the 1850s, the U.S. government had begun seeking ways to pacify the region, remove the Kiowas and other groups from the southern plains, and clear the way for settlement. In 1867, at the Treaty of Medicine Lodge, the Kiowas (along with the Comanches and the Kiowa-Apaches) agreed to settle in southwestern Indian Territory in return for assurances that the U.S. government would curtail the encroachment of illegal settlers on Kiowa land, restrict buffalo hunters (who were rapidly depleting the herds), and provide annuities in the transition to a settled life within the borders of the reservation.[17]

Its promises notwithstanding, the Medicine Lodge Treaty did not solve the so-called Indian problem on the southern plains. In many respects, it only made matters worse. In what William Hagan has called "a mockery of true bargaining," the treaty did little more than "give the stamp of legitimacy to the United States' efforts to concentrate the Indians and open the region to white exploitation." Hagan is correct; a number of difficulties surfaced soon after the Kiowas moved to the reservation, not the least of which was the increasing scarcity of food. There was also an increasingly fractious internal tribal debate about how best to deal with the reservation's appalling conditions. The indiscriminate and deliberate slaughter of the bison herds by white hunters, combined with the government's failure to deliver supplies and annuities promised by the Medicine Lodge agreement, fueled the worsening conditions. In 1874–75 the situation deteriorated into armed conflict in the brief but disastrous Red River War in which the army stormed back into Kiowa country and that resulted ultimately in the imprisonment at Fort Marion, Florida, of thirty-six Kiowa and Comanche headsmen. By the early 1880s, the bison had all but disappeared and the Kiowas had lost their ability to resist the encroachment of white settlers onto their land. One way of life ended, and the Kiowas found themselves compelled to face a period of rapid social and cultural change.[18]

During this same period, Kiowa socioreligious institutions increasingly came under attack by the U.S. government, which launched a campaign to prohibit traditional practices. In 1890, for example, federal officials enforced this directive by terminating with military force the Kiowa Sun Dance—the ceremonial center of the Kiowas' way of life. Thus, by the late nineteenth century, the U.S. government had cleared the way for Episcopalians, Methodists, Presbyterians, Baptists, and Catholics to make significant inroads into the reservation. But in an additive belief system, Kiowa socioreligious traditions were not completely supplanted. Indeed, many Kiowas combined elements of Christianity with their traditional beliefs. Peyotism, for example, evolved from such a combination. By the early twentieth century, peyotism (later designated as the Native American Church) had gained considerable strength among the Kiowas and had spread throughout the plains region. Today, the Native American Church coexists with Indian churches as vibrant and dynamic expressions of Kiowa religion and identity.[19]

In establishing the Kiowa-Comanche-Apache Reservation, the U.S. government sought to open the southern plains for settlement; it also sought to "civilize the Indians" and subsequently assimilate them. But the Medicine Lodge agreement was flawed from its inception. The agents assigned to manage the reservations were rarely qualified, with the exception of the Quakers, and almost never represented Indian interests. The government repeatedly failed to supply the necessary resources for its own programs. It had promised the Kiowas schools at the Medicine Lodge Treaty, for example, and even when Kiowa people and their agents repeatedly requested schools, the government only partially met its obligations. Even the plan to assimilate the Indians as farmers never fully reached its projected goals. By every account, the reservation system failed miserably.[20]

A final blow to the political autonomy of the Kiowas came with the execution of the Dawes or General Allotment Act in 1901 (enacted by

Congress in 1887). Under its stipulations tribal groups would no longer be wards of the government, thus freeing the government from the responsibility of supplying annuities established by treaties such as Medicine Lodge. The Dawes plan entailed allotting tribal members individual plots of land on which they were to become self-supporting farmers. The Kiowas regularly expressed their objections to plans to allot their reservation, and in 1894 they sent a delegation to Washington to air their grievances over the Jerome Agreement, the contract to implement the Dawes Act on their reservation. A number of discrepancies surfaced concerning the agreement, including testimony from the accord's signers, who insisted that they had been misled. In *Lone Wolf v. Hitchcock* (1903), however, the Supreme Court endorsed the federal government's power to allot the reservation. Thus, by the end of the twentieth century's first decade, Kiowa, Comanche, and Kiowa-Apache tribal members had been forced to accept 160-acre allotments, with well over two-thirds of their reservation opened for white settlement.[21]

Using reservations, allotment, education, and Christianization as the keys to assimilation, reformers ultimately intended to end government paternalism by transforming Indians into self-sufficient farmers. The programs, however well intended in Washington, ultimately failed because they were impractical, ethnocentrically conceived, and catered to white goals instead of Indian ones. The effects of allotment, therefore, had lasting social, cultural, and economic effects on the Kiowas, compounding their difficulties and increasing their dependency.[22]

By the 1920s, reformers and bureaucrats alike began to acknowledge that the government's assimilation agenda had largely failed. The 1928 Meriam Report—a comprehensive review of the country's Indian policy—exposed a host of scandalous abuses and prompted an outcry for serious change. In 1934, buoyed by the Roosevelt administration's Depression-era experiments, Commissioner of Indian Affairs John Collier crafted an "Indian New Deal" that encouraged economic stability, political recognition, and spiritual rehabilitation. Initially inapplicable to the Oklahoma tribes, Collier's plan was soon included in the Oklahoma Indian Welfare Act of 1936. Under its provisions, the Kiowas, Comanches, and Kiowa-Apaches organized an intertribal business committee to handle joint tribal affairs. For a time, the business committee also functioned as a de facto political unit until it dissolved in the late 1960s.[23]

The 1950s saw a brief restoration of assimilationist policies under the rubric of "termination," but by the early 1960s the War on Poverty, with its emphasis on economic development, ushered in a new eagerness to amend past wrongs to Indians. Native American peoples were encouraged to participate in government, especially in the Bureau of Indian Affairs. A new emphasis on the rights of tribal polities to handle their own affairs began a new dialogue for self-determination and tribal sovereignty that continues to this day.[24]

Encouraged by the political activism of the 1960s, the Kiowas, Comanches, and Kiowa-Apaches organized as separate political entities. The Comanches were the first to do so, in 1966, followed by the Kiowas in 1970 and the Kiowa-Apaches in 1972 (who then officially organized as the Apache Tribe of Oklahoma, thus emphasizing their political independence from the Kiowas). Politically and economically, the Kiowa Tribe of Oklahoma now acts independently of the Comanche and Apache tribes. (The exception is the KCA Land Use Committee—a separate legal entity established during the 1970s that manages lands owned by all three tribes.) But socially and culturally, the boundaries between the Kiowas, Comanches, and Apaches are ambiguous given their long history together. Most if not all contemporary Kiowas, for example, trace their ancestry through a complex web of not only Kiowa, but also Comanche and Kiowa-Apache relationships—kin and otherwise. These webs of relationships are further maintained by community institutions such as powwows, hand games, peyote meetings, and churches, all of which uphold to varying degrees the traditional alliances of the last two hundred years.[25]

Part 1 **The Kiowas and Christianity**

3. The Saddle Mountain Kiowa
Indian Baptist Church graveyard.
Photo: Luke Eric Lassiter, 2000.

Clyde Ellis

The Jesus Road at the Kiowa-Comanche-Apache Reservation

In early June 1997, a large crowd of mourners gathered at the Saddle Mountain Kiowa Indian Baptist Church cemetery in southwestern Oklahoma for the funeral of Harry Tofpi Sr. Under a small picnic shelter, huddled against an uncharacteristically cold summer rain, family and friends stood shoulder to shoulder and said their goodbyes to Harry. Others, bundled against the weather, sat in their cars. The coffin was opened for one last viewing; we prayed and sang Kiowa hymns and family songs. About thirty minutes after we arrived, the rain finally let up, and we carried the coffin to the gravesite on the edge of a large family plot. After a final round of prayers and speeches, relatives and friends lowered the coffin and filled the grave. We adorned the mound with flowers and several small American flags, lingered for a moment, and then drove back to the Tofpi homeplace south of Carnegie, Oklahoma, where we shared a meal and celebrated the memory of the man whose passing had drawn us together.

To most observers, Harry Tofpi's funeral looked like a garden-variety Baptist affair. The events that filled the hour or so we spent in the cemetery at Saddle Mountain were solidly Christian in intent and expression; even the mourners who used the occasion to talk in the Kiowa language did so to invoke the promise of resurrection and redemption according to mainstream Christian belief. Jesus, God, and heaven were repeatedly mentioned, as they often had been during the days just prior to the funeral. Indeed, Harry's grave is in the very shadow of a large wooden cross that rises some eight feet out of the ground and is one of the cemetery's most visible and dominant features. He is surrounded, moreover, by hundreds of graves that bear irrefutable witness to the importance of Christianity in the Kiowa community.

Even in the cemetery's oldest corner, where the graves date from the first decade of the twentieth century, rich expressions of Christianity's transformative power are everywhere. Tombstones with carvings of Bibles, crosses, scripture, and images of Jesus reflect a sense of Christian identity that often puzzles outsiders, who express surprise that Kiowas did not resist conversion as being inconsistent with their Indian ways. Yet the proof of something more profoundly complicated can be found in every row of graves. This is Christian ground, plain and simple. In this cemetery it is possible to begin to grasp what Vincent Bointy meant in a 1998 interview when he said, "Those old people really *believed* it and they lived it." Cornelius Spottedhorse agreed: "Those old people *meant* it. They had powerful words, prayers—miracles happened. I hear a lot of stories."[1]

But Saddle Mountain is also a place that reminds us that those who are buried there died as they had lived—as Kiowa people. This cemetery and a dozen others like it spread throughout Kiowa country in southwestern Oklahoma are powerful evidence of how Christianity has helped to shape Kiowa belief, ritual, and identity during the last one hundred years. For many Kiowas—as for Indian people generally— Christianity has been, and remains, a crucially important element in their lives as Native people. Its concern for community needs, its emphasis on shared beliefs, and its promise of salvation have helped to mediate life in a region long buffeted by limited economic development, geographic isolation, and cultural stress. This was especially true when the first missionaries entered the Kiowa-Comanche-Apache Reservation in the 1870s as the vanguard of a movement designed to root out every vestige and aspect of Indian culture and replace it with another one based on solidly white, middle-class values. Faced with the inescapable reality of rapidly changing social and cultural circumstances, the Kiowas found their traditional spiritual moorings threatened. Though a variety of nativistic alternatives appeared in the decades to come—the Ghost Dance and Native American Church, for example—many Kiowas found solace in new forms of belief and worship brought by the half dozen Christian denominations that opened missions on the reservation. In the end, many Kiowas agreed with Big Tree's wife, Omboke, who put it this way more than a century ago: "The Jesus Way is the best way for Indians to travel." [2]

But taking the "Jesus Way" is not necessarily the story of how one set of beliefs replaced another one wholesale, or of the incompatibility of Kiowa practices with Christian ones. Rather, it is a more complex encounter in which both sides made concessions. As Stumbling Bear, a Kiowa, once reminded Methodist missionary J. J. Methvin, the "white man's road . . . [is] good, better than [the] Indian road. But not *all* of the ways of the white man [are] better than *all* the Indian ways. Some Indian ways [are] best." [3] Harry Tofpi's gravesite rites, for example, were the culmination of a series of ritual and spiritual events that reflected both his Kiowa heritage and his life as a Christian. Raised as a Christian, Harry was also a lifelong member of the Native American Church and often said that he felt closest to Jesus in the peyote tipi. Like many of his contemporaries, Harry had little trouble reconciling Christian ways with Kiowa belief and practice. On that rainy day at Saddle Mountain, traditional Kiowa ways were expressed through a Christian lens that revealed permeable cultural practices deliberately adapted to fit new forms and needs. Matters were further complicated by the fact that his Sac and Fox relatives on his wife's side mourned him according to their ways, which included a meal for friends and family, a singing, and an all-night wake on the grounds of the family home in Meeker, Oklahoma. A Christian service in the parlor of the Tofpi home in Carnegie came the next day, followed that evening by a peyote meeting sponsored by the Kickapoo and Kiowa chapters of the Native American Church.

Early the next morning, we loaded Harry's coffin into the back of a pickup truck for the short trip to Saddle Mountain. The emphatically Christian beliefs and rituals that occurred during the four days of grieving following Harry's death were no less Kiowa than Christian; indeed, many people argue that they are Kiowa ways *because* they are Christian ways. And they were no less Christian despite being heavily imbued with Kiowa symbols, rituals, and actions. Christianity is not a zero-sum encounter in Kiowa country; it rarely is in any place or at any time.

Humanity and Christian Philanthropy Will Rescue Them

The road to Harry Tofpi's funeral service began in the nineteenth century, when the U.S. government committed itself to a program of Indian assimilation driven by Christian philanthropists as much as by public policymakers. As Francis Paul Prucha has noted, the notion of transforming Indians according to specific cultural agendas rooted in the church was standard fare beginning in the colonial and early national eras. Early in the history of the republic, "[i]t was quietly understood, by government officials as well as by church leaders," writes Prucha, "that the American civilization offered to the Indians was *Christian civilization.*" By the middle of the nineteenth century, missionaries represented what Robert Berkhofer Jr. has called "an integrated social system, an entire blueprint for living which structured institutions and the roles individuals played in them." Thus, Christianity and civilization were opposite sides of the same coin; in striving to convert Indians to Christianity, Berkhofer noted that missionaries would also "teach them to live like white people."[4]

Eager to help shape the republic's national identity in the early and mid–nineteenth century, "[m]issionaries worked more than ever," writes Henry Warner Bowden, "on the assumption that one set of cultural standards—the one shared by churchmen and politicians—promoted both spiritual progress and national stability. They took it for granted that Christianity undergirded republican virtue. . . . Religious principles were supposed to pervade all facets of national experience, including the Indians." Indeed, as one missionary put it, he was "entirely unable to separate religion and civilization."[5] According to the mood of the day, because separating the two would have distorted both beyond recognition and compromised the very integrity of the agenda, this notion of separation struck missionaries as irrational. As a result, even before the hyper-Christian impulse that defined Indian policy after the Civil War, church leaders were marching in lockstep with policymakers.

The relationship between official Washington and the churches, alas, did not provide the relatively quick and painless absorption for which Thomas Jefferson, Henry Knox, and others had so fervently hoped. Indeed, it did little to prevent the calamities of removal and more often than not was used as a justification for the dispossession of Indians, not their transformation. But the fact that Christian missions did not solve the Indian question by midcentury did not end their influence. Public faith in a Christianized Indian policy remained high, especially in the post–Civil War trans-Mississippi West, where church leaders shortly found themselves once again at the center of Indian policy. And given the rapidity with which the line of settlement was moving westward, there was an urgent need for a policy that could balance the Americans' rapacious appetite for land with Indian rights. As Commissioner of Indian Affairs Nathaniel Taylor admitted in 1867, American expansion was not only crowding Indians, it would "soon crush them from the face of the earth, unless the humanity and Christian philanthropy of our enlightened statesmen shall interfere and rescue them." Two years later, the Board of Indian Commissioners announced that "[t]he religion of our blessed Savior is . . . the most effective agent for the civilization of any people," and he called for schools, missions, allotment, and an end to treaty making.[6]

Alarmed by what Robert Keller describes as "desperate violence in Indian-white relations" resulting from the flood tide of expansion and Indian resistance by the 1860s, policymakers turned again to Christian philanthropy, making it the cornerstone of federal Indian policy in the decades to follow. Congressional committees and private reformers alike excoriated the federal government's miserable performance and issued fist-pounding demands for improvements. The congressional Doolittle Committee reported in 1867, for example, that Indian policy could hardly be anything except the disaster it was in light of the fact that the Indian Office was a sinkhole dominated by "the most outrageous and systematic *swindling* and *robbery*." For its part, the privately funded Indian Peace Commission (authorized by President Andrew Johnson in 1867) reported one year later that while the Indian question was of "momentous importance," "[n]obody pays any attention to Indian matters."[7]

Both reports concluded that the Indian question should be in the hands of reformers who would embrace the hard work of transforming Indians and resist the lure of getting rich off of the system's spoils. Responding to the often-heard demand that the Indian Office be transferred to the Department of War, both reports adamantly refused to support the move. The Doolittle Committee ruefully admitted that although the Indian Office was riddled with employees who were "inefficient, faithless, and even guilty of . . . fraudulent practices," it expressed little confidence that the army could do better. For its part, the Indian Peace Commission minced few words when it noted that "not one in a thousand [soldiers] would like to teach Indian children to read and write, or Indian men to sow and reap." Moreover, because the Indian Office was so crippled by what it euphemistically called "bad men" and compromised by the conflicting interests of military and civil authorities, the only solution was that it be "committed to an independent bureau or department" beyond the reach of the party hacks who had soiled their hands at the public trough. The answer, according to the

Peace Commission, was "the hitherto untried policy in connection with Indians, of endeavoring to conquer by kindness."[8]

The solution to this sorry state of affairs had profound consequences for the Kiowas. The details took several years to smooth out, but the impetus appeared in late January 1869, when a group of Quakers met with president-elect U. S. Grant to urge his support for "an Indian policy based on peace and Christianity and the selection of religious employees for the agencies as far as practicable." Grant, rumored to have replied, "Gentlemen, your advice is good," requested a list of like-minded Quaker men suitable as agents and with the words that gave the name to his administration's policy, closed the meeting by saying, "Let us have peace."[9]

In his subsequent 4 March 1869 inaugural address (which included a grand total of two sentences concerning Indians), Grant's hope for a policy that "tends to their civilization and ultimate citizenship" was already more or less on the drawing board. This expression of the president's thinking was the opening for which reformers had been waiting, and shortly after the inauguration, William Welsh—a man Robert Keller characterizes as "the nation's most aggressive Indian reformer"—summoned a group of Quakers and other philanthropists to Philadelphia for a meeting. They petitioned Grant for an official role in Indian policymaking, telling him that while the Indian Office was certainly entitled to its own approach, "without the co-operation of Christian philanthropists the waste of money would be great, and the result unsatisfactory." In late March, Grant and Secretary of the Interior Jacob Cox met with yet another delegation that comprised various denominations and, as Prucha puts it, "accepted their ideas." Smitten by the lure of church-sponsored Indian reform, within three weeks Congress approved the creation of the Board of Indian Commissioners to oversee policy.[10]

In his first annual message, delivered in December 1869, Grant lamented the "continuous robberies, murders, and wars" against the Indians and called any attempt to exterminate them "too horrible for a nation to adopt without entailing upon itself the wrath of all Christendom." The answer, he said, lay in a system of reservations staffed by civilian agents who could teach Indians to live "within the limits of civilized society." In all, during 1869 the Grant administration reaffirmed the historic role of the church in Indian policy, endorsed the fundamental recommendations of both the Doolittle Committee and Indian Peace Commission reports, and "set post–Civil War Indian policy ever more firmly in the pattern of American evangelical revivalism." Indeed, notes Prucha, by the early 1870s, the Peace Policy could just as easily have been called the "religious policy." [11]

Determined to solve the Indian question peaceably, Grant quickly invoked the support and cooperation of the country's churches. Events unfolded with increasing speed as philanthropists, reformers, and various church associations began to clamor for their share of the spoils. It did not take long. Beginning in 1869, most of the nation's western Indian agencies were doled out to various Christian denominations. In 1872, the commissioner of Indian affairs reported that 239,899 Indians at seventy-three agencies were now the responsibility of twelve denominations and the American Board of Commissioners for Foreign Missions. [12] The Kiowas did not know it, but the Quakers — and shortly thereafter the Baptists, Methodists, Presbyterians, Catholics, Mennonites, and Episcopalians — were headed their way as the representatives of official policy.

The Peace Commission brought its commitment to church-sponsored reform to Kiowa country in 1867, when it held treaty councils with the southern Plains tribes at Medicine Lodge, Kansas. The Kiowa-Comanche-Apache (KCA) Reservation created by the subsequent treaty was assigned to the Central Superintendency, a region that included much of the Indian Territory and parts of Kansas. Assigned to the Orthodox Friends, or Quakers, the superintendency's ten agencies held 17,724 Indians, including some 1,900 Kiowas. (The ten tribes assigned to the KCA Reservation had a combined population of 5,490 in 1872.) Stretching across an area the size of Connecticut, the reservation quickly gained a reputation as a place that was difficult to administer and even more difficult to control. This situation did little to endear its tribes to federal officials, many of whom agreed with Secretary of the Interior Columbus Delano's 1871 assessment of Kiowas and Comanches as "predatory and criminal." The commissioner of Indian affairs was equally appalled by those tribes, which he described in 1871 as having "caused the greatest trouble during the past year." And while he took aim at the Comanches and Apaches for their resistance, he specifically assailed the Kiowas for their "gross outrages," "restless and war-loving spirits," and "passion for plunder."[13] From the beginning, the agency's extreme conditions tested the Peace Policy as thoroughly as anywhere in the country. And if a policy based on prayer, Christian fellowship, and humanitarian reform could prevail there—in a place where in the words of one critic "wild Indians seames [*sic*] to be running at large with out restriction"—it could work anywhere.[14]

In May 1869 the Kiowas got their first Quaker agent, an earnest, forty-seven-year-old Iowa farmer named Lawrie Tatum, whom the Kiowas immediately dubbed Dan-pa-ingya-t'ai, or Bald Head. The living embodiment of the Peace Policy, Tatum eschewed force, relying instead on "heavenly wisdom, sufficient for the . . . business devolving upon me." Though he once described the Kiowas and Comanches as "probably the worst Indians east of the Rocky mountains," he also thought of them as wayward children who needed only gentle but firm instruction. "My trust was in the Lord, who could restrain the evil intentions and passions of the Indians," wrote Tatum. Thus "the witness of God in their hearts would be reached" and even the most irremediable soul saved. Tatum was convinced that the blame for the mess in Indian country lay not with the tribes but with unscrupulous white settlers. Indeed, in the spring of 1870 he insisted that raids attributed to the Kiowas and Comanches had actually been carried out by whites disguised as Indians. As it turned out, things were not that simple. At any rate, as William Hagan has noted, "there was no more incongruous spectacle than that of a Quaker agent preaching the virtues of peace and agriculture to a plains warrior, treating this man . . . as a simple, misguided soul who could be brought to see the error of his ways by compassion and sweet reason."[15]

Tatum spent the next four years struggling against impossible odds. Three months after arriving, for example, his requests for supplies for the Kiowas alone exceeded what had been promised to the entire group of tribes that had signed the Medicine Lodge Treaty. (The Indian Office turned him down cold.) He also needed more staff. The treaty had stipulated only one agency farmer for the 3.5-million-acre KCA Reservation, so Tatum promptly requested twenty-six more, plus an additional fourteen cooks, and noted that those numbers would need to be increased in the coming year to eighty and thirty, respectively. The Indian Office declined every request. As a result, the agency nearly collapsed in the spring of 1870 when chaotic conditions prompted every Quaker employee except for one couple to resign and flee; one month later Tatum's own wife left.[16]

More than anything, the Friends were unprepared for the complete inadequacy of a church-based policy to control a reservation whose inhabitants were distinguished by a strongly martial culture. By all accounts, the frequency and brutality of the region's violence, and the seemingly casual attitude of Kiowa and Comanche raiders toward their victims, stunned Tatum. In June 1870 alone, for example, a white farmhand was killed and scalped near Fort Sill, a teamster was shot in front of Tatum's home, and another man was murdered in Beaver Bridge. One year later, the infamous Warren Wagon Train raid occurred, ultimately leading to the convictions of and death sentences for Setainte, Setangya, and Big Tree. (The death sentences were later commuted to life imprisonment.) Between 1871 and 1872, Kiowas killed at least twenty Texans, and Tatum reported that the Kiowas described their victims as "marks for Indians to shoot at." When Tatum begged the Kiowas to stop raiding, Setainte told him that if the whites wanted them to stay out of Texas, they should move it farther away, where the Kiowas could not find it.[17]

Reinforcements arrived in 1871 when Quaker missionary Thomas C. Battey assumed control of the boarding school (later renamed Riverside) recently established by fellow Quaker A. J. Standing at the neighboring Wichita Agency. But if he brought renewed energy to the field, Battey was perhaps a bit too pious for the task at hand. He walked the last twenty-three miles to the Kiowa Agency, for example, separating from his traveling companions "when his conscience would not permit him to listen any longer to their continuous swearing." A man who could not condone garden-variety swearing was not likely to be comfortable with the rough edges of agency life. In 1872, Battey left Riverside for Kicking Bird's camp to open a school and administer the gospel. There, good intentions notwithstanding, he ran into hard times. As Quaker agent James Haworth tersely noted in his 1873 annual report, "Thomas C. Battey has not been very successful in keeping up a school." The Kiowa Agency's first boarding school finally opened in 1873, when Ohio Quakers Josiah and Elizabeth Butler established a small school near Fort Sill attended primarily by Comanches and Caddos. Six years after Medicine Lodge, government schools were still nowhere to be found, and there were no missions.[18]

By then, both the Quakers and the Peace Policy were in serious trouble. As early as 1870, Tatum had disappointed (and infuriated) his superiors by writing that the only way to control the Indians was to "whip them" with seasoned troops. In 1872 he admitted that "the Kiowas . . . are uncontrollable by me." Tatum resigned in 1873, exhausted by the level of violence, repeated threats to his life, and the government's endless capacity for failing to meet its obligations. His tenure was an omen of things to come. Only two Quaker agents (Tatum and Haworth) were assigned to the Kiowas, and when Haworth was replaced by P. B.

Hunt, an Episcopalian, in 1878, both the Quaker era and the Peace Policy were dead in the water.[19]

The failure of the so-called Quaker Policy became apparent during the Red River War of 1874–75, in which Kiowas, Comanches, Cheyennes, and Arapahos struck white settlements. The attacks rekindled old hatreds on the southern plains and prompted brutal retaliatory raids by the army. Federal officials began to rethink the Peace Policy. As one wag put it, "Give us Phil Sheridan and send Phil-anthropy to the devil." Tellingly, sentiment in the East (where the Peace Policy had previously found warm support) began to turn against a policy that relied on what one newspaper ridiculed as "soft-soaping Quakers." Another warned that "a Kiowa will wear a Quaker hat, but he will never carry a Quaker head." By 1879, agent Hunt's annual report indicated a profound shift at the reservation. Twelve years after Medicine Lodge, he wrote, there were not only no permanent missionaries on the reservation, but little support or encouragement for them. It was a harbinger of things to come. For much of the next decade, there were no permanent missions on the KCA Reservation.[20]

In 1887, however, the passage of the General Severalty Act—widely known as the Dawes Act, or allotment—brought renewed urgency to the role of the church in Indian policy. As discussed in the introduction, the Dawes Act called for the division of reservations into 160-acre homesteads. Once it was completed, allotment would signal the end of Indian country both physically and psychologically by literally erasing the boundaries that defined reservations. Moreover, advocates promised that allotment would not only liquidate reservations, it would also liquidate Indian culture by forcing the tribes into the American mainstream. There would be no more Indian country and thus, no more Indian problem. "Reformers looked upon the Dawes Act as a major milestone in their crusade to solve the Indian problem," writes David Wallace Adams. According to Adams, "In a single piece of legislation they believed they had found the mechanism to smash tribalism, transform hunters into farmers, and grant the Indians U.S. citizenship."[21]

Moreover, the problems of the Peace Policy aside, the image that policymakers had for Indians remained firmly anchored in mainstream Protestant ideology. Along with allotment and schools, missions constituted an equal partner in a new holy trinity on which policymakers now placed their hopes. And although the allotment of the KCA Reservation would not occur for more than a decade, the time was at hand to renew the partnership between missionaries and federal policy that would solve the Indian question once and for all. As Methodist missionary J. J. Methvin put it, "[C]ivilization alone does not civilize. . . . a veneering of civilization may be given or forced upon a people and yet leave them void of the real purposes and high aspirations of life and it soon wears off." It was "the Gospel, faithfully preached," Methvin once wrote, that "not only saves [the Indian's] soul, but qualifies him for taking on the habits of civilization." [22] The time had come to pave a new Jesus Road into the heart of Kiowa country.

The Jesus Road in Kiowa Country

We have the light now. Do not be ashamed to follow Jesus.
Big Tree, at his baptism, 1893

Armed with a renewed sense of importance, and backed by a new federal policy based on the rapid absorption of Indians, missionaries flocked to the KCA Reservation in numbers that eclipsed anything the Kiowas had ever seen. Indeed, only one year after the Dawes Act was in place, Agent E. E. White hailed the rising tide of mission work. "One hopeful indication for these Indians," he wrote in his annual report for 1888, "is the interest now being manifested in them by religious societies and mission boards. During the past year three missionaries have entered this field and others see the greatest opportunities which it presents. . . . It is my policy, as I understand it to be yours," he concluded, "to encourage all religious and missionary societies in their work among the Indians." [23]

By the time White wrote his report, the Baptists and Methodists were already in the saddle. Before long, the roll call of KCA mission stations and schools was a lengthy list of American churches. The Reformed Presbyterian Church of North America, the Methodist Episcopal Church South, the American Home Baptist Mission Society, the Board of Home Missions of the Presbyterian Church in the United States of America, the Territorial Baptist Convention, the Catholic Order of St. Benedict, the Women's Board of Missions of the Methodist Episcopal Church South, the Dutch Reformed Church, the Women's Auxiliary to the Domestic and Foreign Missionary Society of the Protestant Episcopal Church, the Mennonite Brethren Church of North America, the Women's American Baptist Home Missionary Society, the Women's Executive Committee of the Reformed Church in America, and the Women's Baptist Home Mission Society of Chicago were all there in one form or another. The only major American denomination missing was the Mormons, whose otherwise keen sense of proselytizing did not extend to Indians. By 1900, there were nineteen churches on the KCA Reservation.[24]

By far the most influential denominations on the reservation were the Catholics, Methodists, and Baptists, each of which brought a different strength to the mission field. The Catholics opened a highly successful mission and school at St. Patrick's in Anadarko, for example, but they did not duplicate the extensive network of stations that the Baptists and Methodists built in the years between 1887 and 1913. The Baptists were notable for the numbers of devoted women who ran their stations. Indeed, the role of women at all of the KCA missions was extraordinarily important, but the Baptists excelled on that count. The Methodists were enormously successful at bringing Kiowas into the ministry, as evidenced by the fact that nearly a dozen of the first generation of converts were ordained. Although the Episcopalians, Mennonites, and Presbyterians opened missions and schools, in the long run they did not maintain a significant presence among the Kiowas.

Among the first to arrive were the Catholics. In early 1888 the Catholic Indian Bureau expressed its interest in establishing a mission and school on the reservation. Buoyed by earlier successes in the Indian Territory with the Osages and Poncas, the Catholics were experienced and committed. In the fall of 1891 Father Isidore Ricklin arrived in Anadarko with his mule, Stub, and began a thirty-year career in Kiowa country that even his Protestant contemporaries acknowledged as one of the most notable in the history of the reservation. Ricklin ran an especially successful boarding school, a fact that the Indian Office appreciated, given its own chronic inability to meet the requirements of the Medicine Lodge Treaty.[25]

Shortly after his arrival, Ricklin petitioned the government for 160 acres for a mission station under the auspices of the Catholic Indian Bureau. With the generous support of Philadelphians Mother Katherine Drexel and Archbishop Patrick Ryan (who was also a director of the Catholic Indian Bureau), construction began one year later at a site one and a half miles south of Anadarko. The school, named St. Patrick's in honor of the archbishop, opened on 25 November 1892 with thirty-five students and a cadre of six teachers from the Sisters of St. Francis. The mission itself opened one month later.[26]

The Catholics were especially interested in opening a mission school, and they poured great energy into it. Indeed, enrollments grew so rapidly that a new wing was added in 1893; three years later, St. Patrick's held 106 students, twice the capacity of the Methodist and Presbyterian schools combined. Efficient and clean, St. Patrick's had a devoted and dependable staff, avoided the dreaded outbreaks of trachoma and other diseases that plagued the government schools, and was run so well that it became something of a showpiece at the KCA Reservation. "In its heyday," notes Benjamin Kracht, "St. Patrick's mission consisted of two dormitories, a classroom building, laundry house, rectory, and home for the sisters. A large farm . . . produced adequate food for the students, and the surplus was sold for cash. After 1901, Father Isidore had a dairy barn constructed and milk was delivered into town on a regular basis." [27] No government school then in operation on the reservation came close to matching such a standard.

Ricklin moved easily in the Indian community and quickly gained the confidence of Comanche and Kiowa headsmen in the Anadarko area, a feat that produced tangible results. On 12 February 1893, for example, when St. Patrick's held its largest mass to date, a contingent of Kiowas and Comanches listened patiently to a visiting bishop's lesson about the sacrament of baptism. They then made their own prayers and offerings, which included a plea from the Kiowas for more "great spiritual men" who could teach them "to live rightly." Taking a more practical point of view, a Comanche asked for "better luck with their ponies and . . . pastures." One writer later observed that "[i]t was a memorable day, during which much spiritual good was afforded the assembled Indians and which augured more favorably the destiny of St. Patrick's mission." [28]

Like most missionaries, Ricklin also opposed practices that he believed were contrary to the Kiowas' needs. On one occasion, for example, he confronted a group of Ghost Dancers. As Jack Hokeah remembered the event in a 1968 interview, "I was watching him and he put up his altar where they always had the Ghost Dance. And he put on all those . . . vestments that they always wear when they say the mass. . . . [H]e got them on and then he started just the way the Catholic priest says the mass—from the start to the last and then when he got through, he took off his robes and put them back together and ever since . . . they didn't have a Ghost Dance, and maybe, I thought, maybe somehow through the powers of God, he ended that Ghost Dance." [29]

The flush times were not permanent, however. The opening of the reservation in 1901 under the provisions of the Dawes Act brought an influx of Catholic homesteaders, and Ricklin was forced to divide his time between St. Patrick's and the new Holy Family Church that he opened in Anadarko in January 1902. More than that, the government had already begun to phase out support for contract schools, which meant that St. Patrick's lost its enrollment-based subsidies. The school survived, but most of the other mission schools did not. By 1920, St. Patrick's and the Presbyterian school at Cache Creek were the only mission schools in operation, and Cache Creek was in its last years. Moreover, on 1 December 1911 the Bureau of Indian Affairs assumed control of St. Patrick's and renamed it the Anadarko Boarding School. The government hired Ricklin and the Sisters of St. Francis to administer the school, but from that point on it no longer operated under the auspices of the Catholic Church. Ricklin remained in Anadarko until his death in 1921, an occasion marked by the fact that on the day of his funeral every business in Anadarko closed its doors. The boarding school he started in 1892 finally closed in 1963.[30]

Ricklin made the Catholic Church a force to be contended with, but because he did not establish permanent Indian missions or schools outside of Anadarko, Catholic influence was negligible in the reservation's more isolated districts. And it was in those corners that the Methodists and Baptists made their mark. One of the first churches to make a commitment to the KCA Reservation in the years following the Dawes Act was the Methodist Episcopal Church South, whose most illustrious missionary was John Jasper Methvin, a forty-year-old Methodist minister who arrived in Anadarko in late 1887. Of all the missionaries to the Kiowas, none, save Ricklin and the Baptist Isabel Crawford, left a comparable legacy. In an interview two decades after Methvin's 1941 death, Eugenia Mausape, a Kiowa who had attended both the Methvin mission and school, was brief and to the point: "Great man, J. J. Methvin." Today his memory survives in Anadarko at the J. J. Methvin Memorial United Methodist Church, where his legacy is perpetuated by a small but devoted congregation.[31]

In 1886 Methvin made what he called a reconnoitering trip to the KCA Reservation, which he described as inhabited by "wild tribes" that were "feasting and gambling and racing by day and indulging in their wild orgies by night." His impression of the agency was equally vivid. "The Agency itself was in a chaotic state," he remembered. The agent had been removed, the school superintendent was a drunk, and "things were in a stir." All in all, he concluded, "it was a crude and crusty crowd." In other words, the KCA Reservation was ripe for mission work, but Methvin did not anticipate getting the assignment. "Inasmuch as I had a wife and five young children I did not judge myself eligible for so difficult but glorious a task. So I was startled into quickened heartbeats when I heard Bishop Gassoway in his clear, musical voice read 'Missionary to the Western Tribes, J. J. Methvin.' " [32]

Methvin settled in Anadarko in 1887 and turned his attention south of the Washita River, where Methodist efforts had been restricted to whites, he noted, "to the neglect of the Indian. This will be our chief danger for the future." In 1889 Methvin—whom the Kiowas called A-mi-a-me, or Ant-shaped Man—applied for, and received, several parcels of land on which to establish churches and a mission. The Board of Missions of the Methodist Episcopal Church South built a parsonage and church on a two-acre lot in Anadarko and provided Methvin with twenty-five hundred dollars for a boarding school, also in Anadarko. The school, which stood just south of present-day Central Boulevard in the Highlands Addition, opened in 1890 with an enrollment of thirty-four Kiowa, Caddo, and Wichita students. Methvin enlarged the school in 1891 to accommodate one hundred students. By 1892 he added a sixty-acre farm and livestock operation. Of the fifty-one students enrolled that year, thirty-three were Kiowas. The Women's Foreign Missionary Society of the Methodist Episcopal Church South assumed control of the school shortly after it opened, and in 1894 the group renamed it the Methvin Methodist Institute. [33]

The early emphasis on mission schools was deliberate, for like every other missionary, Methvin considered schools a crucial component in the civilizing agenda. Incorporating what David Wallace Adams has called "a larger vision of national destiny," policymakers and mission-

aries designed Indian schools to promote Protestantism, individualism, and Americanization. Thus, because spiritual elevation and cultural transformation were mutually reinforcing elements, Methvin, like
Ricklin, devoted enormous amounts of energy and resources to the mission schools. As Forbes noted, the stakes were clear to Methvin, as in
1893 when he wrote that "[a]s a race they are doomed. . . . [T]he white
man, designing, aggressive, persistent, is on every hand, and right in
their midst. . . . [T]hey must take on the spirit of his progress or go down
before it. With their present life the latter is inevitable." Christian education (and, even better, *Methodist* education), would liberate the Indians. Eight years later, continues Forbes, Methvin remained unequivocal
about the proper course: "There can be no preservation of the Indian as
an Indian. He must be absorbed into the great body of American citizenship." Christian education, therefore, was a moral imperative: "For
Methvin, Christianity provided civilization its heart, its ideals, its staying power." Without it, he said, the Kiowas did not stand a chance. Indeed, at his retirement in 1907, Methvin suggested that the Kiowas had
escaped literal extinction only because of "what the Gospel has done for
these people." In this he found common ground with Commissioner of
Indian Affairs Thomas J. Morgan (1889–93), who was a Baptist minister
himself and a professional educator. Extolling the virtues of a common
school education, Morgan once wrote that in combination with "the
solace and stimulation afforded by a true religion," education would
"convert them into American citizens."[34]

In addition to the hard work of educating Indian children, Methvin
also spent a great deal of time in the Kiowa camps, where he assisted
the government's field matrons, who taught everything from hygiene
to quilting. "The principal work of these women," wrote Methvin, "has
been to visit the families in their homes, teach the women how to do
things in domestic civilized home life, read the Bible, hold prayer meetings, etc., and thus, while improving their home life, reach them with
the message of the Gospel." Methvin also sponsored large camp meet-

ings, a practice that reflected both Methodist and Kiowa traditions of extended religious gatherings. Realizing that short services were inconsistent with many traditional Kiowa practices, Methvin believed that extended camp meetings could eventually replace the social, cultural, and spiritual functions of the Sun Dance encampments and all-night peyote meetings. Indeed, some of the hallmarks of mission work on the KCA Reservation in the decades to come were the annual conferences, camp meetings, and revivals at which hundreds of Indians camped for weeks at a time, just as they had in earlier days.[35]

Once in the camps, Methvin encountered some of the same practices that had compelled Ricklin to take to the field in an aggressive show of force. Whereas Ricklin opposed the Ghost Dance, Methvin thought that the rising influence and popularity of peyote posed the greatest threat to his work. Much to his dismay, a fairly large number of Comanches and Kiowas were staunch advocates of this new, pan-Indian religion, which Methvin denounced as "nature worship" and "a drug habit under the guise of religion." He was especially annoyed by James Mooney's overt support of peyotists at the agency and referred to Mooney as "a crank" and "a representative of the Ethnological Department of the Smithsonian Institution . . . [who] was a persistent enemy of any effort by church or state for the civilization and Christianization of the Indians." And as Bruce David Forbes points out, Methvin made a point of mentioning in his published works that not only was Mooney openly supportive of peyotism, he was also a Catholic and, by definition, worthy of suspicion.[36] His crusade notwithstanding, Methvin did little to erode peyote's popularity.

Gaining the confidence of the Kiowas was a slow and often laborious process, and like every missionary in Indian country, Methvin needed help translating the gospel into Native languages. Methvin relied heavily on interpreters, but he also tried to learn the Kiowa language, an effort that occasionally backfired. Kiowas tell a story to this day of a Methvin sermon during which he said in Kiowa that Jesus came into town "on his ass," using the word that refers in English to burro. In Kiowa, however, the words for burro and ass are not interchangeable. When they heard Methvin's choice of words, his listeners erupted in a torrent of giggles, muffled conversations, and rib-poking. Methvin's colleague, Rev. B. F. Gassoway, had his own problems on this count. When he began shaking his fist and shouting during one sermon, his listeners "arose and solemnly filed out of the building" because, as one man later said, "he is mad at us." On another occasion Gassoway was leading a Comanche congregation in the Lord's Prayer with the help of an interpreter; all was going well until he reached the phrase "give us this day our daily bread," at which point the congregants picked up their belongings and headed for the noon meal.[37]

Like other missionaries, Methvin was rescued by the interpreters who came to his aid. Working in the Mount Scott area, he recruited Virginia Stumbling Bear and, later, Laura Pedrick and the Mexican captive Andele. Methvin singled out Andele for his ability to defuse the skepticism that Kiowas often displayed in his presence. Calling him "[t]he most remarkable character with whom I have been associated in my mission among the Indians," Methvin regarded Andele—who was eventually ordained—as "a greater force for the uplift of the Indians than any other force in their midst." At one especially troublesome meeting, Methvin remembered that Andele "took the leadership in his own hands, and poured out upon them an exhortation of such pathos and power that the whole wild element came pressing to the front, and falling in the attitude of prayer and supplication . . . [m]any turned from the old way, and started on the new, and all opposition for the time died." Before long, Methvin reaped a harvest of conversions, including Luther Sahmaunt, Jimmy Quoetone (father of Guy Quoetone, himself a future Methodist minister), Hunting Horse and his sons Albert and Cecil (both future Methodist ministers), Sankedota, Howard Sankedota, and Apeahtone.[38]

With Methvin as their model and inspiration, the Methodists made headway. By 1890 there was a Fort Sill circuit, and in 1891 Helen Brewster went to the Little Washita, where she opened a mission for Comanches and Mexicans. By 1897, there were at least six Methodist missions on the KCA Reservation: the original two-acre tract in Anadarko, the Methvin Institute, the Mount Scott Kiowa Methodist Church, the Cottonwood Grove Methodist Church (near Verden), the Little Washita Mission, and a small parsonage and chapel at Fort Sill. The first four served Kiowa communities, and the latter two were with the Comanches. New stations were subsequently added at Cedar Creek in 1911 and Hog Creek in 1913.[39]

By the turn of the twentieth century, however, the Methodists began to lose momentum. Several things contributed to this situation. The government's earlier decision to end its support of contract schools placed new financial pressures on all of the mission stations, many of which relied on the subsidies for their survival. Moreover, the growing emphasis on transferring Indian children to public schools raised doubts about how long mission schools should be maintained. Indeed, one of the first mission schools to close under the weight of these conditions was the Methvin Institute, which was sold in 1907 for forty-five thousand dollars to an Anadarko land syndicate. Calling the decision to close the school "a heart breaking sight," Methvin assailed the buyers for their "vile misrepresentations," "spirit of avarice," and "cupidity and greed," but he was powerless to stop them. "It was an evil day for the church and community," he later wrote. "Here was an opportunity to build a great school that would have been a blessing for the future generations. . . . Oh, the tragedy of it." Methvin was so disheartened by the setback that he retired one year later.[40]

The institute's closing was one of a series of closely spaced disappointments. In 1906, for example, the Methodists abolished the Oklahoma Methodist Indian Mission Conference in the belief "that Indian Methodism should be absorbed into the white churches." The Fort Sill mission closed at about the same time, and the Anadarko mission was in dire straits. Worse, the Methodists suffered the ire of KCA agent Ernest Stecker, with whom they became embroiled in a series of arguments.

The spat began when Rev. B. F. Gassoway attempted to revive the Methodists' presence, especially in Anadarko. Stecker, however, mounted what Gassoway perceived to be a vendetta based on the agent's personal dislike of the Methodists. In June 1909, for example, Stecker tersely informed the commissioner of Indian affairs that the original two-acre Anadarko mission was "a very old and dilapidated one and should be torn down and moved away. In its present uninhabited state it only invites Indians of low character to assemble there." (Stecker was also apparently angered by the fact that the run-down site was an eyesore fewer than one hundred yards from his own residence.) On the cusp of losing the site, Gassoway prevailed only when Cato Sells (commissioner of Indian affairs from 1913 to 1921) informed Stecker that the mission could remain in operation as long as the church wished to support it.[41]

So the Anadarko mission survived, but the Methodists continued to lose ground. Disgruntled by the Indian bureau's decision to maintain the Catholic St. Patrick's boarding school (which he mistakenly took to be a rebuke of Methodist efforts), Gassoway repeatedly lodged complaints with agent Stecker and made thinly veiled comments about the agent's pro-Catholic stance. Annoyed, Stecker dismissed Gassoway's remarks as "degrading . . . rash statements having no foundation in the truth." (Methvin could not resist the occasional barb, either, as when he once pointedly referred to "the Catholic school near Anadarko, supported by the Government.") Stecker stood his ground and, on at least one occasion in 1913, appeared to mount a counterattack. Well aware of the Indians' practice of spending Sundays camped on the mission grounds, Stecker "had all the land adjacent to the [Anadarko] Mission premises brought under the plow," wrote Gassoway, "leaving the Mission in the midst of a cultivated field, with an outlet some fifteen feet wide . . . and no space at all to camp or even hitch teams."[42]

Gassoway consulted the congregation, and together they concluded that "it would suit them better under the changed conditions to erect another place of worship some distance from town, more convenient to their homes and with ample camping grounds." This situation apparently influenced the decision to establish churches at Hog Creek and Cedar Creek and a day school at Mount Scott, where there would ultimately be two Methodist mission stations—one each for the Kiowas and Comanches. The Methodists maintained most of their KCA mission stations, but after 1907 they focused their attention on the rural districts outside of Anadarko. In 1918, after losing more than half of their Indian members, the Methodists reestablished the mission conference, but control over finances and property remained under the control of non-Indians.[43]

By then, the damage had been done. In the early 1940s, in fact, there were no Indian Methodist churches in Anadarko. By the mid-1940s, however, Rev. Ted Ware, a cofounder of the Hog Creek Chapel (later Ware's Chapel), organized the J. J. Methvin Memorial United Methodist Church. Interestingly, Kracht reports that the district superintendent for the Oklahoma Indian Mission Conference thought the idea was so hopeless that he told Ware, "You cannot do it. If you do, I'll eat my hat." Undeterred, the congregation met in private homes, at a Methodist church in town (which eventually turned them out), and finally, in an old creamery in downtown Anadarko. In the fall of 1945 the congregation moved into its own building in east Anadarko near the fairgrounds. That building was subsequently replaced by the present facility in 1965.[44]

By the middle of the century, the Methodists had regained their footing. In 1963 the Methodist Church estimated that it was reaching nearly half of Oklahoma's 123,000 Indians; 1 of every 16 Indians, it claimed, was enrolled in a Methodist church. In 1972, the Oklahoma Mission Conference became the Oklahoma Indian Mission Conference. As of the year 2000 there are 7,200 members worshiping in eighty-nine churches in Oklahoma, Kansas, and north Texas. The effort pioneered by Methvin in 1889 grew to eleven churches during the twentieth century: Albert Horse, Apache, Botone Memorial, Cache Mission, Hunting Horse, J. J. Methvin, Little Washita, Mount Scott Kiowa, Mount Scott Comanche, Petarsy Mission, and Ware's Chapel (formerly Hog Creek).[45]

At about the same time that Methvin and the Methodists were beginning their work, the Baptists initiated an enormously successful, longlived mission program.[46] As with the other denominations, the Baptists had been in the region for several decades, working for the most part among the Five Civilized Tribes in the eastern half of the Indian Territory where, as one missionary put it, "the field is white to the harvest and the laborers few." Missionary Isaac McCoy preached the first Baptist sermon to the Plains tribes in about 1825 at Union Mission in present Wagoner County, but like Methvin he was discouraged by his church's ambivalent commitment to Indian missions. "I feel not a little ashamed of the Baptist denomination," wrote McCoy in 1831. There were "about three hundred thousand Baptists in the United States," he continued, "and none so much regarding the wretched Indians as to come and collect them into a fold and administer them the ordinances." Forty-five years later, A. J. Holt uttered the same lament when he reported that there were thousands of "wild Indians" at the KCA Reservation but no Baptist churches.[47]

This dearth was partially explained by the fact that a good many people remained convinced that the KCA Reservation was a place somewhere near the edge of the earth inhabited only by wild tribes and desperately isolated missionaries. Persuading people to come to such a place was no easy task. George Williams, whose daughter accepted a job in 1896 at the Rainy Mountain Boarding School, had to ask the KCA agent where, exactly, Rainy Mountain was, for none of the railroad maps in Ohio showed its location. Unable to locate the nearest railhead—which was seven miles north of Rainy Mountain, at Gotebo— Williams asked for "some directions to Anadarko, it is a long distance and a strange land." Ten years later, another employee wired the agency to say "as Gotebo cannot be located by any railroad agent nearby, I will go to Anadarko." One woman who accepted a job at Rainy Mountain confided to a friend that "I am in hell." And when Isabel Crawford was assigned to Elk Creek in 1893, she recorded two initial impressions in her diary. The first was that she expected to be scalped within twenty hours; the second (and more troubling, apparently) was that Elk Creek was "87 miles from the railroad!"[48]

When a carpenter turned lay preacher named W. D. Lancaster and his wife established a school and mission in Lone Wolf's camp in 1889, most observers later referred to that event as the true beginning of Baptist missions among the Kiowas, who called Baptists *onbop,* which means "to immerse." Working without a commission, Lancaster was supported in part by Rev. W. F. ReQua, an itinerant missionary from the American Baptist Home Mission Society who was convinced that "some of the Kiowa[s] . . . want to be Christians and be baptized." In the spring of 1891 Lone Wolf requested more missionaries. "I want to see you," went his message. "Come now! I want you to tell me what I and my people must do."[49]

Veteran Baptist missionary J. S. Murrow arranged a meeting with Lone Wolf and Big Tree twenty miles west of Anadarko. Also in attendance was a contingent of American Baptist Church missionaries, including Rev. G. W. Hicks (a North Carolina Cherokee), Lauretta E. Ballew, Henrietta Reeside, and Mrs. M. C. Reynolds, who was the corresponding secretary of the Women's American Baptist Home Mission Society. The meeting was long remembered for Lone Wolf's speech (which the church never tired of reprinting), in which he explained the Kiowas' willingness to accept the missionaries. God had divided the world into two seasons, said Lone Wolf, warm and cold: "You Christian people are like the summers. You have life and warmth and growth. We poor, wild Indians are like the winter. We have no growth, no knowledge, no joy, no gladness. Will you not share your summer with us? Will you not help us with the light and the life, that we may have joy and knowledge and eternal life hereafter?"[50]

Encouraged by the notion that the Kiowas wanted missions "right where their people lived," in October 1892 the American Baptist Home Mission Society (whose officials found Lone Wolf's appeal "urgent and touching") authorized Ballew, Reeside, and Hicks to establish missions at Elk Creek and Rainy Mountain for the Kiowas, and at Quanah Parker's camp for the Comanches. Their concern for the Kiowas was genuine, but the Baptists also saw an opportunity to steal the march on the Methodists and Catholics. "Let Baptists be the first to build a chapel among the Kiowas," wrote Murrow, and "not in the white settlements." Hicks shared this feeling, but he was also driven by a compulsion to counter Catholic influence. "If the Romanists can see the good of putting up a $30,000 school building here," he wrote in 1892, "most surely the Baptists ought to build up a strong school." After discussing the matter, the Kiowas announced their willingness "to let our friends have 160 acres for the mission." Quanah was also willing to let the Baptists build a mission in Comanche country and told them to "select a place wherever you want it." But Quanah was not especially enthusiastic about having the Baptists as neighbors (he preferred the Mennonites) and reportedly told Hicks to make sure the site "is not close to me here."[51]

Hicks, who had baptized Lone Wolf, Omboke, Gotebo, and eight other Kiowas the previous winter in Anadarko, opened the Lone Wolf Mission near Hobart in the spring of 1893. Lone Wolf, who had previously lamented the fact that "the old people put us on the wrong road," was now "full of joy and gratitude." "The red people need not be behind the white people," he said, but with the help of the missionaries "might go side by side." Such hopes were significantly strengthened in May when Big Tree asked for baptism. A Ghost Dancer and ardent opponent of missions, Big Tree was best known for his role in the notorious 1871 Warren Wagon Train massacre. Given his adamant stand against the missionaries, he seemed an unlikely convert, so his baptism was a significant victory for the Baptists. (It was also a difficult one. Owing to his size—340 pounds—the event required two men to handle the immersion.) "We have the light now," Big Tree said during the camp meeting at which he was baptized. "Do not be ashamed to follow Jesus now.

He is a good road, the only road. . . . Turn to his road, follow Jesus and do not be afraid or ashamed." [52]

Until the Elk Creek and Rainy Mountain stations were built, Ballew —whom the Kiowas called Ma-ta-ma, or One Who Shows How to Do— and Reeside—known as Aim-de-co, or Turn the Other Way—lived at the Wichita Agency and drove or rode to the Kiowa camps. "At first we had no house of worship," Reeside wrote, adding that "often the boughs of trees formed the roof under which the gospel was taught." Much like the federal government's field matrons (Ballew, in fact, left the mission field to become one in August 1895), they dispensed medicines, organized quilting bees, prepared meals, and held prayer services—often with the help of "large colored pictures to illustrate our simple story of Jesus and his love and death for us. Before long we were well known in many camps and lodges." Big Tree, Gotebo, and Lone Wolf were steady supporters, remembered Reeside, and "with their families drove up as regularly as white people would [to] go to church." [53]

But it was an uphill battle on many fronts. Many Kiowas remained openly skeptical of the missionaries and kept their distance. Ernestine Kauahquo Kauley recalled her grandmother's stories in which the Elk Creek Kiowas ridiculed and teased Reeside and Isabel Crawford. "These two dedicated women were horrified at the thought of the Indian men and women gambling and squandering their money, all their possessions, by just gambling," Kauley remembered. "They would walk among the people and cry, and the Indians thought it was very funny; because they were wasting their time, and they called these two dedicated women 'the poor, crazy old white women.'" Crawford and Reeside, however, turned the tables when they agreed that in order to reach the Kiowas, they would have to follow St. Paul's injunction to go and live with the unbelievers, which meant taking on the local customs. To that end, they camped with the Indians, ate their food, and alas, "even gambled with them in order to win their confidence," according to Kauley.[54]

4. Rainy Mountain Mission around the
turn of the twentieth century. The original
chapel is on the right. Courtesy, American
Baptist Historical Society.

As with the Elk Creek mission, the Baptists secured a 160-acre tract at Rainy Mountain, where Hicks, Ballew, Reeside, and thirteen Kiowas organized a mission in January 1894. Hicks conducted services on alternate weekends at Elk Creek and Rainy Mountain (also called Immanuel Mission); Ballew and Reeside filled in when he could not make the trip. By November they had erected a chapel (built with funds collected from Illinois Sunday school classes), and membership stood at thirty. In March 1895 the congregation elected four Indian deacons, including Big Tree, "who is too heavy for active service," wrote Mary Burdette in 1898, but being "gifted in speaking, [he] assists in the meetings." [55]

On 29 March 1896 a new era began when Rev. and Mrs. Howard H. Clouse arrived at Rainy Mountain from Cedar Rapids, Iowa, to assume charge of the station. The Clouses remained at Rainy Mountain for twenty-seven years and were instrumental in establishing subsequent missions at Red Stone in 1896, Saddle Mountain in 1896, and Cache Creek in 1906. Reverend Clouse rode the circuit between missions and provided religious instruction at the nearby Rainy Mountain Boarding School. His wife, Mary, worked with the government field matrons. "Having no children," wrote Robert Hamilton, "they gave their all to the Indians. . . . They were father and mother to the Indians." [56]

In the fall of 1893 a woman arrived at Elk Creek who was destined to become one of the most influential and controversial missionaries ever to work at the KCA Reservation. Isabel Crawford was a twenty-eight-year-old Canadian who graduated in June 1893 from the Baptist Missionary Training School in Chicago. Posted to Elk Creek, she arrived on 23 November with Hattie Everts. Three years later she moved thirty miles east to Saddle Mountain, after local Kiowas asked for their own mission. Disgruntled by what he perceived as a lack of attention, one Saddle Mountain Kiowa pointedly grumbled that "Lone Wolf and Big Tree got the churches, but the Indians live over here." Crawford established a flourishing mission with the assistance of Lucius Aitsan, who with his wife Mabel served as her interpreters, sponsors, and occasionally as her protectors. Educated at Carlisle, Aitsan had interpreted for other missionaries, including the Catholics, but said that the priests spoke so quickly that he could not keep up with them. Aitsan was ordained in 1913 after serving many years as a deacon, but he perished in the 1918 influenza epidemic.[57]

Frail and nearly deaf—the Kiowas called her T'-aw-kama, No Ears, or Woman Who Is Hard of Hearing, and later Gee-ah-hoan-go-mah, She Gave Us the Jesus Way—Crawford forged a relationship with her congregation that was unique on the KCA Reservation. Mary Aitson's father-in-law, who knew Crawford, remembered her as "a brave and courageous little woman." Though fiercely determined to make the Kiowas thoroughly Baptist, Crawford was also willing to meet them in the middle. "No white Jesus man ever sat down with us," said one man. "You, one white woman, all alone among Indians and no scared—this is good. We like this." She proved especially adept at understanding the importance of feeding and caring for the community, and her willingness to endure privations of the worst sort endeared her to the congregation.[58]

Crawford was especially successful at using Baptist rituals of baptism and burial to introduce and encourage new practices. One Kiowa recalled that Crawford bridged the distance between the Kiowa sweat lodge and Christian baptism by heating rocks that were then dumped into the baptismal pool in a stream above the church. Like her Mennonite colleagues at the Post Oak Mission (with whom the Saddle Mountain Kiowas shared a close and mutually supportive relationship), Crawford realized that "births, baptisms, and burials were their best opportunities to explain to a more receptive audience the Christian view of salvation, death, resurrection, and the promise of eternal life."[59]

But Crawford also believed that the only way to make the missions a success was to "roll up our sleeves to show them how." This view was not a license to treat Indians badly. "We are not here *to boss* the Indians," she wrote in 1898, "but to do what they let us do when it is not wrong. If they are not 'citizens' on earth, they are citizens of heaven and no person has a right to domineer over them." She remained optimistic about the possibilities and wrote at one point, "the Lord, I think, is putting us in a position to push a little. The Indians are progressing nicely—more, perhaps, spiritually than physically, for they make more of an effort 'to catch the Jesus road' than to catch a plow. They never had such opportunities to succeed." [60]

Crawford established a mission where Kiowas maintained a clear sense of control. They built and paid for a handsome chapel that was dedicated in 1903, and they also operated a day school. Like the Rainy Mountain congregation, the Saddle Mountain group elected deacons to direct the work, but unlike the other stations, the Saddle Mountain Kiowas also voted to allow their deacons authority over church rituals and sacraments, a decision that the other missions had largely resisted. Headstrong and outspoken, Crawford clashed repeatedly with Clouse over doctrinal interpretation. Matters reached a breaking point in 1903 and 1904 when she became embroiled in an acrimonious battle with Clouse over the congregation's decision to allow Lucius Aitsan and the Saddle Mountain deacons to administer communion when an ordained minister could not attend. The mission board forced her resignation in 1906 and barred her from returning to Oklahoma. At her death in 1961, her body was brought back to Saddle Mountain and laid to rest under a stone with the inscription "I Dwell Among Mine Own People." Her grave lay at the head of the cemetery that she and her first converts had begun more than sixty years earlier. [61]

The Baptists proved especially good at organizing, and in 1897 they established the Oklahoma Indian Baptist Association. Ten years later, it had a membership of 777 from eleven churches spread across the Kiowa, Comanche, Cheyenne, and Arapaho communities. In order to streamline the work, the association was divided in 1917 into two divisions. The churches west of the Rock Island Railroad—which included the

5. Saddle Mountain Kiowa Indian Baptist
Church, 1903. Lucius Aitsan is in the upper
left-hand corner. Courtesy, American Baptist
Historical Society.

KCA missions—were sponsored by the American Baptist Home Mission Society and organized themselves into the Western Oklahoma Indian Baptist Association. Those east of the line continued to be known as the Oklahoma Indian Baptist Association. As with the Methodists, however, Indian control of the work eventually slipped away; in 1934, all mission work in Oklahoma was turned over to the Home Board of the Southern Baptist Convention. As a result, many Indians in southwest Oklahoma felt as if they had lost a voice in the administration of their own church affairs.[62]

Choosing a Road

I have been asking Jesus on the sly
to send a Jesus woman to our district
and to my home that I might learn more.
Lucius Aitsan

It is tempting to dismiss Christianity as a force that duped unwitting Kiowas into selling out their culture and their identity in favor of something that was antithetical to their lives as Indian people. Of course, trading their original culture for something entirely foreign to them was exactly what the white missionaries wanted the Indians to do. But part of the irony here is that Indian-led mission associations often spoke out against dances, peyote, and other practices that they deemed unacceptable. In 1904, for example, the Oklahoma Indian Baptist Association issued this unambiguous statement: "We cannot follow the Jesus Road and other roads at the same time. Let us lovingly try to win them back to follow Jesus' road only. If they will not follow the Jesus road . . . then Jesus says we must cut them off." Five years later, the same association insisted that "we do not believe the Ghost and Peyote Roads are good ones, because we, the true Christians, have found the Jesus Road so much better." Omboke, Big Tree's wife, expressed it this way: "I do not know about those of our fathers who never heard of the Jesus Road, but if we who have heard of it turn away from it, we will have no one but ourselves to be blamed." [63]

Resistance to the missions was stout, however, and it came from influential corners. Sun Dance advocates, for example, kept the dance going until 1887, when the army finally suppressed it. Even as the Sun Dance was faltering, though, other movements appeared. In 1882, a young man named Datekan announced a vision that directed him to bring back the buffalo. He took a new name, Pa-tepte—Buffalo Bull Coming Out—and began making medicine. His hopes notwithstanding, he was not especially successful. Five years later, however, in 1887, Pa-ingya—In the Middle—revived Pa-tepte's vision and claimed "the power to resurrect the dead and to destroy his enemies with a glance as by a lightning stroke." Prophesying the destruction of the whites and unbelieving Indians, he promised a final cataclysm in the spring of 1887 that did not occur, and "the excitement died out." [64] But it was followed almost immediately by the Ghost Dance, the most powerful nativistic movement on the plains in the late nineteenth century.

The Ghost Dance represented a profound threat to the message being spread at the missions. In the fall of 1890 the Arapaho Ghost Dance prophet Sitting Bull visited the Kiowas and held a ghost dance on Rainy Mountain Creek that was attended by nearly the entire tribe. One year later, the Kiowa Apeahtone visited Wovoka, the Paiute man responsible for the spread of the dance. Unimpressed, Apeahtone returned home and denounced the ritual as a fraud. But its followers were determined to maintain the dance, and Kiowas practiced it until well into the twentieth century. For some Kiowas, the Ghost Dance was a logical alternative to the gospel, as Isabel Crawford learned in 1896 when she confided to her diary that a Kiowa Ghost Dancer told her "the Great Father talked to us Himself, and told us He gave the Book to the White people and taught them to read it, but He gave the Indians the dance road and told us to hold on to it tight till He came to earth with our dead and the buffalo." [65]

Peyotism also posed a serious challenge to the missions. Increasingly widespread after 1880, peyote was a nativistic response that combined traditional practices with new rituals, including Christianity. Like the Ghost Dance, peyote was a direct response to the ennui of reservation life. Unlike the Ghost Dance, however, it was not a messianic movement but an accommodative one. Moreover, the public support of acknowledged experts like James Mooney lent it credence and legitimacy. That some of its forms also contained more than a veneer of Christian doctrine did much to disarm critics, even though the federal government kept up its opposition through the twentieth century. Across the KCA Reservation, the years between 1880 and 1930 were characterized by a chronic battle between missionaries and peyotists.[66]

Yet all of this discussion begs the question of why, and how, the Kiowas found room for Christianity. What would convince them to take on these ways? As Forbes notes, there was much in Christianity that was in theory uncompromising when it came to conversion. In the best of times, missionaries might see Kiowa religion "as a sort of Old Testament faith, worthy but needing the completion of the Christian gospel." At worst, "anything not clearly the work of the Christian God must be a product of opposing Satanic power."[67] Either way, there seemed to be little middle ground.

For their part, some Kiowas were mystified by both the theological peculiarities of Christianity and by the various denominations' competing claims as the one Christian truth. In some cases, the Kiowas' questions were of a practical bent, as in October 1900 when a man named Henkey asked Crawford, "Does the Jesus Book say that Christians should carry revolvers? Many of the Christians are buying them and carrying them around. White people are coming. I want to know what the Jesus Book says." (Crawford replied that it was not right for Christians to carry guns.) On other occasions, the questions confronted the welter of faiths represented on the reservation, something that troubled some Kiowas. In November 1901, one man asked Crawford, "Why did the Great Father give out so many Jesus roads, Catholic, Methodist, Presbyterian, Baptist? Why did He scatter us like that? Why didn't He make one strong Jesus road?" After some discussion of the matter, he offered a solution. "In the middle of the summer let us call a big council and get in all the Methodists, Presbyterians, Episcopalians, Catholics, and their missionaries and you talk to them from the Book and look into their eyes and don't give up till you beat them. Then we will make one big strong Jesus road and all the Kiowa Christians will walk on it, for we want to please Jesus only." Crawford, if nothing else a dyed-in-the-wool Baptist, coolly replied, "It is not a wise road." [68]

Yet the question remains. Why did so many Kiowas accept Christianity? Several things are suggestive, including the influence of leading Kiowa figures (especially Native ministers and interpreters), the effectiveness of missionaries (especially women), the role of the church in establishing and maintaining community identity, and by the mid-twentieth century a more tolerant attitude that made plural expressions of faith and belief more common. Above all, there is the reality that accepting Christianity did not mean agreeing to the end of Kiowa identity and culture. Moreover, whatever the particular details, it is important to note that the Kiowa experience was not at odds with the larger history of Christianity in Indian country, where similar forces and accommodations were always at work. As Raymond DeMallie notes in his work on the Lakota Black Elk, for example, Black Elk's conversion was both spiritually sincere and culturally grounded in Lakota needs and practices. "Christian churches," DeMallie writes, "provided institutional structures that were not merely tolerated but encouraged by the government, allowing communities to organize themselves, with leaders and spokesmen who could represent their interests. . . . Church activities helped structure reservation life and provided individuals with avenues to achieve respect and attain influence. By the early 1900s, almost all Lakotas belonged at least nominally to one or another Christian denomination." [69]

Other tribes had similar experiences. Kenneth M. Morrison points out that Montagnais people accepted Catholicism for both ideological and material reasons in a process that revealed the deeply syncretic nature of the encounter. As in the case of the Kiowas, Morrison reminds us to reconsider what exactly "conversion" meant from a Montagnais point of view. James Ronda's work on colonial New England raises the same issue, and Clara Sue Kidwell's work on the Choctaws makes strikingly similar points about why Kiowas accepted Christianity. Churches in the Choctaw community flourished not because they limited the expression of Choctaw ways but because they reinforced them. In the late nineteenth century Choctaw remained the language spoken in church where, for example, it "provided a new voice for Choctaw leadership" and found renewed expression in hymns and traditional songs. "Choctaws could come together at churches in ways that were familiar," notes Kidwell, and though missionaries tried to suppress traditional ways, the churches became a focal point "as places where they could congregate and be themselves, where they could speak their own language and visit and play stickball." [70] Much of this culturally flexible Christianity would be adopted by the Kiowas.

The missionaries' need to gain the support of leading men and women in the Kiowa community was perhaps the most crucial element of their work. Without the overt participation and backing of these people, missions generally failed. Thus, winning the approval of key leaders was always a primary objective. At the KCA Reservation, every denomination succeeded in persuading a core of important men and women to follow the Jesus Road. Once that happened, according to missionary Ioleta McElhaney, a Kiowa, others followed: "If the leader, the one who is the leader of the camp . . . keeper of the lodge, or keeper of the household . . . , if he chose to follow a way, then the others would follow suit. Not by force, but because he is wiser and they look to him. And if he sees that it is good, well then they would want what he has." [71]

So when Big Tree, Lone Wolf, and others spoke out in favor of the missions, they did so as chiefs and headsmen whose opinions mattered.

Because of Lone Wolf's stature, for example, his statement that "the old people put us on the wrong road" was a powerful one that could not be easily dismissed. Members of prominent families carried influence, as when a man named Odlepaugh joined a delegation of Baptist Kiowas to preach at a Ghost Dance camp in 1904. Odlepaugh was a charter member of the Saddle Mountain church and, more importantly, the son of Setainte, arguably one of the most famous nineteenth-century Kiowa leaders. (Of those listed on the roster of charter members printed in Crawford's memoir, Odlepaugh alone was singled out for his family connection as "Odlepaugh, son of Satanta.") Speaking to a childhood friend at the ghost dance he hoped to break up, Odlepaugh said, "I had a very bad temper and hurried up to get mad always. You see I am getting over it. I go to the Jesus House and listen, and listen, and listen, and I try, and try, and try and it is Jesus and His Holy Spirit who are helping me." Because this statement came from the son of Setainte, Ghost Dancers would have been hard pressed to dismiss it. Lakotas heard a similar plea from Black Elk in 1907, when he asked them to "show respect to the priests who live with you and obey them, and hold on to what they tell you and stand firm."[72]

The conversion of high-profile members of the tribe was evidence to all that Christianity could fit in their world. A particularly revealing story in that regard concerned Hunting Horse, a one-time peyotist. In 1967, at age seventy-six, his son Cecil gave an account of his father's conversion in 1900:

My father became religious in the white man's way. It so happened that he went blind. . . . And he didn't know what to do, only to worship the "Great Spirit" as he calls it. So he asks some of the people to take him up to the mountain, that is called Mt. Sheridan. . . . And he told them not to come to see him till after four days. That he was gonna do some sacrificing and worshiping and the Great Spirit . . . would give him his eyesight back. . . . It so happened that on the fourth night—the last night—something talked to him, [saying] that at day break he was going to get a blessing. . . . Toward the last, as he opened his eyes, he looked out to where his home was at. And he saw the house. . . . And there . . . he became religious, he said he has found God. . . . So he went to the missionary J. J. Methvin and told him that he wanted to be baptized, because the Great Spirit had given his eyesight back to him. . . . He became a great leader in the . . . Methodist Church. . . . and he has taught all of his children to become Christians. And it so happened that two of his boys, Rev. Cecil Horse and Rev. Albert Horse, become ministers in the Methodist Church. And then all the rest of the children . . . were baptized, some in the Baptist Church and in the Methodist Church.[73]

Others had similar experiences. The Presbyterians and Baptists, for example, gained the assistance of Joshua and Julia Given, the children of Satank, a contemporary of Setainte and a highly admired nineteenth-century leader. Likewise, J. J. Methvin converted both Tsait-kop-ta, who had been imprisoned at Fort Marion for his prominent role in the Red River War, and Dohausin, the son of a great war leader who had followed his father in the same pursuits. And as Sidney Babcock wrote, when Dohausin asked for baptism, "[m]any Indians who had followed their Chief in war followed him into the church." And in a striking turn of events, when Dohausin was on his deathbed, his tipi was moved to Methvin's backyard so that the old man could die in the company of his missionary friend.[74]

Odlepaugh and Hunting Horse spoke of a new era that demanded changes from the Kiowas. "The old roads are passing away," one Kiowa man said in November 1900. He continued, "How glad I am that I was not born a long time ago. I remember the war-path and the buffalo. . . . Now how different it is. How thankful I am that Jesus sent the missionaries to tell us the gospel. The old roads are passing away; how happy the Jesus road is." In a 1967 interview, Ernestine Kauahquo Kauley expressed a similar idea. A-que-quoodle, her great-grandmother (and Lone Wolf's wife), "lived during the days of the final surrender, and she, too, knew in her heart that the Kiowa would never go back to the warrior days, and taking up Christianity she composed a song [a hymn]. . . . 'My God, I pray to you, oh hear me. My God, I pray to you, oh hear me. How tired my spirit and soul. Let God's Spirit come unto me.' And this is the song that A-que-quoodle left with her grandchildren and her great-grandchildren. And now her great-great-grandchildren also know this song."[75]

Other important factors that influenced many persons to convert to Christianity included the training of Kiowas as ministers and missionaries. Beginning with Joshua Given's ordination by the Presbyterians, a long line of Kiowa men accepted pulpits in the Kiowa Baptist and Methodist churches. In the first generation of converts alone, the Methodists ordained Kicking Bird the younger, Guy Quoetone, Cecil Horse, Albert Horse and his son James, and Andele. As Forbes notes, for Methodists as well as for all the denominations, "such native leadership was crucial." The ordination of Lucius Aitsan as a Baptist minister in 1913 was followed by that of Sherman Chaddlesone and at least two others, all from the Saddle Mountain congregation. George Hunt and his daughter Ioleta Hunt McElhaney became Baptist missionaries in the 1940s. At all of the churches, Kiowas were elected deacons, elders, and lay leaders. J. J. Methvin had anticipated the need for such cultural brokers, and he hoped to provide for them by opening a "Bible and training class with such Indians, both male and female as I can get interested in the matter and give them such training as will make them efficient in telling the story of Jesus as they go out among their own people. I hope to accomplish much in this way in permanent good."[76]

Accounts of missionaries in Indian country often emphasize the religious workers' corrosive effect on Native culture and their antagonistic attitude toward Indians, and it is true that missionaries typically intended to completely transform their converts. The KCA Reservation was no exception. Methvin, Crawford, and others routinely lamented "savage" and "uncivilized" Kiowa practices, and they intended to erase them down to the last detail. Methvin, for example, saw nothing worth preserving in Kiowa culture. "As a race they are doomed," he wrote. "They must take on the spirit of . . . progress or go down before it." But Methvin would not stand for abuse, and he was certainly no exterminationist. Eugenia Mausape remembered that "J. J. Methvin told the teachers and the employees 'Don't be mean to the Kiowas. We're staying on their land and we treat them nice. Treat them nice. If they don't know the lesson, they'll learn it some day. Don't switch them and don't slap them, no. No. It's not right to treat . . . children [that way]'—Oh, it was so nice. Great man, J. J. Methvin." Crawford reminded her readers that missionaries had no right to boss the Indians, and Mennonites A. J. and Magdalena Becker were notable for "their identification with the Comanche people."[77] From the beginning, the KCA tribes were in the company of missionaries whose personal devotion to the Indians' welfare was both genuinely and openly expressed.

At Saddle Mountain, Rev. Perry Jackson, who arrived in 1928, was highly regarded as a minister and for his considerable skills as a carpenter, electrician, and all-around handy man. "Mr. Jackson looked on Indians as human beings," wrote Sherman Chaddlesone in 1942. "He even helped some of our Indians in making homes; he built their houses and barns. . . . He put all his heart and mind in the doing of it. . . . He was indispensable in times of help and in times of sickness. . . . The good things he left us will never be forgotten." Chaddlesone thought so highly of Jackson and his wife that he gave his own Kiowa name—Mipauta, Higher Than the Other, a reference to the Kiowa Sun Dance poles—to the Jacksons' son, Lawrence.[78] Vincent Bointy and Cornelius Spottedhorse recalled how Jackson encouraged attendance by promising free gasoline to drivers based on the number of persons they brought to church on Sunday mornings, a tactic that led to fierce competition between drivers who raced one another over the dirt roads in the campaign to get willing souls.[79]

Female missionaries enjoyed an especially close relationship with the Kiowas, and it is fair to say that much of the early success at the missions must be attributed to women. Why this is so is not entirely clear, but several things seem suggestive. Because most of the men with whom the Kiowas dealt were acting in an official government or military capacity, it is not unlikely that levels of suspicion were high on that count. Suspicions about whites in general were heightened following the opening of the reservation to settlement. "White people are dangerous," said one man. "[T]hey laugh at us and will come with sticks and revolvers and act crazy. The road is hard." Women were almost always the first missionaries whom the Kiowas met, and for whatever reasons, Indians warmed to them quickly and fairly easily. Although they often teased and tested them, the Kiowas were also impressed with the determination of the women, who for their part lived in the Kiowa camps, ate their food, and endured the privations of life on the plains with impressive strength.[80]

Recall that shortly after Crawford's arrival at Saddle Mountain one Kiowa man said that "[n]o white Jesus man ever sat down with us." Also, after being told that the Baptists were sending for more Jesus women, Setainte's widow said, "Tell my white sisters that Satanta's woman . . . loves them . . . [and] loves Jesus. Tell my white sisters we say many times thank you." More than was usually the case for the men, women missionaries enjoyed a sense of inclusion and membership in the Indian community that simply defies easy description. There was, as Marvin Kroeker observes, a deep, gender-based affinity between Indian women and white missionaries reflected in part by the numerous Christian women's societies that appeared at most missions.[81]

Numerous statements appear in the literature about the relationships between women missionaries and their congregations. Shortly after Crawford arrived at Saddle Mountain, for example, the Kiowas informed her that they would no longer call her "white woman" but instead would refer to her as sister. At Rainy Mountain, Reeside and Ballew were so beloved that the locals claimed them as relatives as well. Once, when she repaid a Kiowa for the use of his wagon and team,

Reeside was told, "You need not have done that; I did not expect anything. When your little sister grows up she will not pay me when she uses the horses and buggy. You are my daughter, too, and when you wish to use anything that I have you are welcome to do so." And as much as the Comanches loved Mennonite missionaries A. J. and Magdalena Becker —"They became one of us," said one Comanche man—Magdalena was the one most often singled out for special treatment and respect. Like most missionaries, they were given names, which were deeply laden with meaning. Comanches called A. J. Becker To-sa-mocho, or White Beard, while his colleague and predecessor Henry Kohfield was called Tia-cho-nika, or Little Hat. Magdalena Becker, on the other hand, was called Tah-pah-see, Our Older Sister. She worked ceaselessly in the camps, spoke fluent Comanche (which she also taught to all of her children), and was asked on numerous occasions to name Comanche children. At her death in 1938, she was mourned by a crowd of more than fifteen hundred, larger than that which had attended Quanah Parker's funeral twenty-seven years earlier. At her funeral service Herman Asenap said, "We Indians we loved her. She was just like a mother to us. . . . We Indians, dear friends, feel like Mrs. Becker is one of our Indian people. We love her sincerely." [82]

Likewise, Crawford's death in 1961 at the age of ninety-six prompted an outpouring of sympathy and grief in the Saddle Mountain community. Indeed, the congregation had already told her that when she died, they wanted her body back. In 1927, twenty-one years after she left (and thirty-four years before her death) John Onko told Crawford, "We understand that when you pass on you have arranged to bury yourself here with the Indians. We want these words put on your tombstone: 'I dwell among mine own people.'" At least one other member of the church grumbled about having to wait until she died to have her back: "We don't want you to bring your dead body back. We want you to bring your live body back and stay by it." Today, when Kiowas visit the cemeteries on Memorial Day to clean the graves and visit their relatives, Mary Aitson, who married Lucius Aitsan's grandson, always cleans Crawford's grave. "We always remember her when we go down there. . . . She always seemed like a member of our family."[83]

A final reason for the conversion of Indians was the role played by the churches in nourishing a sense of community identity. Missions were historically located in and around established camps and communities that existed prior to the arrival of whites. Thus, the literature from the period is filled with references to the "Post Oak Comanche Mennonites," "Mount Scott Kiowa Methodists," "Rainy Mountain Kiowa Baptists," the "Hog Creek Kiowa Methodists," and so on. There was some crossing over; Dean Reeder, a white farmer, attended Saddle Mountain Church as a boy and his mother played the piano for services there, but for the most part congregations tended to be either Indian or white.[84]

Once allotment opened the KCA Reservation to settlement, these churches and mission stations became increasingly important as gathering places where Kiowas could maintain relationships. Ioleta McElhaney thought the churches were the natural extensions of traditional Kiowa camps. Commenting on the loss of headsmen and the traditional bands into which Kiowas had once arranged themselves, she said, "[T]oday [1968] we don't have that. We just go helter skelter and we try to make up our own minds. But if we would be in the church, the Lord leads us to make decisions. And that takes the place of that kind of communal life which we had." When asked why Indians tend to go to their own churches, she replied, "I think they enjoy their own fellowship, that's the way they were brought up. Maybe they began first in their own native church. And there's just a better feeling of kinship." When she was a child, her family often attended Mount Scott Methodist, even though they were not formally members of that congregation and were, in fact, Baptists. "We attended because it was an Indian church. In those days . . . we didn't make much of denomination. If our people belonged there, well we would go there, too."[85]

McElhaney's statement reflects a sentiment to which Kiowas return again and again. Helene Fletcher, a Baptist missionary (and Ioleta McElhaney's daughter), remembers from her childhood in the 1940s and 1950s that the churches were rallying points for congregations and the communities in which they lived. People would often camp on the grounds or stay with relatives for several weeks at a time in "old fashioned visits," which invariably included Sunday services that ran all day long with a lunch break in the middle. This form of worship and socializing was especially prevalent during the Korean War, when many families had sons in military service. Services with Kiowa hymns and special prayers often extended into the evening. These services were powerful, Fletcher recalled, adding that she had not been to a similar one since that time. "It was a time when Christianity was important to the church," she said. "Everything was centered around the church. It was important — not the bingo hall, not the dances, not all that other stuff — the *church* was important. It was a very uplifting, a very important part of our lives." The Hog Creek services that Daisey Hokeah attended had a similar impact: "So, all these years we have always known that our church was blessed. When we take our problems to the church they are always lifted, and a lot of miracles happened." Faced with the loss of their church grounds and cemetery due to the expansion of nearby Fort Sill in the 1950s, Comanches at the Post Oak Mennonite Mission called the church a "unifying center of activity" and expressed "a sincere desire to keep this unity of School, Church, Cemetery, and Community." [86]

The churches have also historically been a mediating force in a world that makes demands on Indians to join the mainstream, often at the cost of their traditional tribal values. As McElhaney notes in this work, the church has helped in that transition. One of the greatest strengths of the Becker era at Post Oak was the fact that even if the missionary couple disliked Comanche dances and certain other "worldly habits," "they never insisted that they give up all their Indian ways." Ralph Kotay notes that some people, "when they become Christians . . . want Indians to do away with their traditions. . . . But for me, I won't say that. . . . We even have ministers who are shaking that gourd [gourd dancing at powwows]. You just can't get away from being an Indian." Vincent Bointy suggests that far from denying the role of traditional ways, the church affirms what is best in Kiowa culture by emphasizing the role Christianity plays in promoting and maintaining important practices and beliefs that continued to have meaning in the late twentieth century. "We live in a white man's world," said Bointy, "and to me, the white man's way is not to be Christian." But in his community and family, being Christian is crucial to a Kiowa sense of identity. Indeed, Bointy goes so far as to say that taking on too many white values means losing both their Christian faith and Kiowa identity. Postulating the existence of a Christian worldview that is specifically rooted in Kiowa ways, Bointy stated, "I always said we lost our Christianity because we turned toward the white man's ways." Cornelius Spottedhorse agreed, saying that Christianity is about more than being Indian; it is about accepting relationships with others that embrace what Bointy called *taw'day,* a Kiowa word best translated as "kind" or "generous."[87]

For many Kiowas, the churches helped to maintain these kinds of important values, values that Bointy said transcend being Methodist or Baptist or Mennonite. (The elders "didn't say 'Christian,'" noted Bointy. "They said 'this is the way of God.'") The use of language is a good example. Vincent Bointy said that he believes he can express the power of Christianity better in Kiowa than in English: "You can say so much more." When he visited the graves of his parents and relatives, Harry Tofpi always spoke to them in Kiowa because "that's the language that God gave us, it's the one He understands." As Ralph Kotay and Luke Eric Lassiter point out in part 2, Kiowa hymns are especially important on this count. Bointy noted that Kiowa hymns carry a kind of power and intensity missing in English hymns. "It really tells you how they feel," Bointy said. "You can't get it across in English." Cornelius Spotted-horse added that hymns really speak to the importance of a Christian

life, of love, devotion, and faith: "Those words are powerful in Indian."
In an interesting combination of experiences, it was at Saddle Mountain
that Helene Fletcher heard for the first time not only Kiowa hymns and
prayers but also the spider woman stories that narrate and explain the
earliest times of Kiowa history.[88]

Challenges to Indian Christian Communities
It's a constant battle when you're working for the Lord.
Cy Hall Zotigh, Saddle Mountain church member, 1998

From a historical point of view, it is tempting to see the late nineteenth
and early twentieth centuries as the "Christian" era at the KCA Reservation. In terms of numbers of missions, intensity of the movement,
and levels of influence, it is true that the years between 1890 and 1920
were something of a high tide. By the 1940s, however, a number of internal and external factors forced the churches to struggle as never before.
Changing demographics, the rise of other institutions—especially powwows and the Native American Church—and the loss of the founding
generation of Christian Kiowas brought significant change.

Among the most powerful forces was the migration during and immediately following World War II that took people away from the rural
areas where mission stations had been most effective. Dean and Bell
Reeder, white farmers who have lived in the Saddle Mountain area for
many years, were struck by the steady movement of rural Indians from
the outlying areas into town, a fact that they believe had a devastating
impact on Indian churches, especially Saddle Mountain. This migration
meant the loss, too, of influential and strong leaders who might have led
the smaller churches through the tough times in the 1950s and 1960s.
Cy Hall Zotigh agreed, saying that during the 1940s and 1950s Indian
people moved away from the rural areas in increasingly greater numbers as they left farming for urban-centered jobs that required a move

to, say, Oklahoma City, Dallas, Tulsa, or Wichita. When they returned for visits, he noted, it was for the Indian fairs and dances, not for church events.[89]

Even for those who remained, deep shifts in church culture were already beginning to affect attendance and membership. By 1945 the annual camps and revivals had ceased at almost every church, a circumstance that one Kiowa attributed to the loss of the elders who had established such practices. One of Kracht's collaborators also believed that the shift to wage labor made it impossible for the week-long camps to survive. "You get off work on a Friday evening . . . but we got to get back by Monday morning to go to work. They were free to camp in earlier days," he said.[90]

The decline in numbers was palpable. Membership in the Oklahoma Indian Baptist Association, for example, fell from 1,019 to 821 between 1942 and 1953, a 20 percent drop. Rainy Mountain, Red Stone, and Cache Creek survived the lean years, but Saddle Mountain officially closed in 1963 with the sale of the church and its land. And in more recent decades the churches continued to struggle. The journal of the 1985 Oklahoma Indian Missionary Annual Conference (Methodist) showed membership of 1,167 in six churches but reported that average weekly attendance for all six churches combined was 199, or 17 percent of the membership.[91]

The fairs, dances, and other powwows that emerged after the war years were also a considerable source of conflict for many Indians, especially younger ones who had not grown up in the church. As Morris Foster points out, in the Comanche community the powwow crowd became increasingly influential by the 1950s and used their rising popularity to forge new community-wide traditions that were more attractive to younger Indians. As early as the 1930s, according to Foster, powwows were one of "two distinct 'religions'" in the Comanche community. The other was peyote. As a result, "powwows provided these younger Comanches with their first opportunity to participate actively in a Comanche-derived . . . gathering. Dance gatherings, which previously had had a carnival atmosphere, became more solemn occasions in the late 1930s."[92]

Benjamin Kracht reports that Kiowa elders have told him that in the years since World War II "powwows serve as a religion for the youth." Cy Hall Zotigh attributed the absence of young Kiowas in the churches to the persuasive appeal of powwow culture. People will drive a long way to get to a powwow or peyote meeting, he observed, but not for church. "I'm fighting the dance people," Zotigh said. "[T]hey let it get in the way of God."[93] Another Kiowa suggested to Kracht that "a lot of younger Indians are confused today. . . . We wonder why the younger generation doesn't go to church. But this is a problem. Things have died out over the last forty years. A lot of our younger people don't really know what church is." Zotigh said that "we're deeper than confused. We don't care for one another." As Vincent Bointy put it, after World War II, "they got their prayers answered and they didn't go back [to the churches]." And when they did, it was "like the white people"—only on special occasions. Bointy chuckled about a story in which a Kiowa minister who looked up to see a full house on Easter told them that he was mighty glad to see them and that he would look forward to seeing them again, at Christmas. Ioleta Hunt McElhaney, the Kiowa who served as a missionary at Saddle Mountain in the late 1940s and early 1950s, saw a darker side to the decline. "I think alcohol, the problem of drinking" had led young Indian people "to immoral living, just loose living," she said.[94]

Yet despite these setbacks, Christianity remains deeply important in the Kiowa community today. As in many non-Indian and Indian communities alike, it struggles to maintain its influence, but there is no doubt that for a great many Kiowas, Christianity is a fundamental part of their culture and world. While it is true that the numbers of church-attending Indian Christians are not especially high, using that as evidence of Christianity's nominal influence—as some scholars have done—is to miss a much more complicated set of encounters in which space, community, and belief are worked out.[95]

But the argument that Indian Christianity is not sincere because its numbers are small defines and assigns meaning based on criteria that are not always relevant in the Kiowa community. It also obscures other values, ideals, and encounters at work in the Kiowa community. This is not to say that mainstream Christianity has routed all other forms of belief; the Native American Church is quite strong in the Kiowa community, and traditionalists, powwow people, and a small but energetic group of Pentecostal and Holiness followers are also part of the community's discourse about religion and spirituality. Yet at most public forums, community gatherings, powwows, and other ritual and ceremonial gatherings, there is clear and convincing evidence that Christianity has become a vital part in the core of contemporary Kiowa culture.

Above all, there is a deep and abiding concern for the welfare and well-being of Kiowa people. Cy Hall Zotigh said that he lived every day of his life trying to be like Lucius Aitsan and Isabel Crawford. "Love everyone," he said, "rich and poor. Love and show concern about people, no matter who they are. Being a Christian is having the love of God in your heart and in your life." And those are values that Vincent Bointy said remain at the center of being a Kiowa. "Those old people, they emphasized be good to other people. They didn't say 'Christian.' They said 'this is the way of God.'" In gatherings of all sorts in Kiowa country, that ideal is borne out at hymn singings, powwows, church meetings, family reunions, baptisms, and funerals. It is especially powerful in the cemeteries at Hog Creek, Rainy Mountain, Red Stone, Anadarko, Carnegie, Saddle Mountain, and a half dozen others—the cemeteries where the collective memory of the Kiowa people has been laid to rest for the past one hundred years. There, in the shade of cedars, in the clutching embrace of the constant prairie winds, surrounded by the monuments and crosses, it is clear that, as Cornelius Spottedhorse put it, "it's really sacred ground. God is real." [96]

And that is why Harry Tofpi wanted to be buried there, because he was a believer, and he said that he knew Jesus would be in that grave-yard when his time came. But he also said that his grandpa and grandma would be there, too, waiting on him, waiting for their Kiowa boy to come home.

Part 2   **Kiowa Hymns**

6. J. J. Methvin Memorial United Methodist
Church. Photo: Luke Eric Lassiter, 2000.

Luke Eric Lassiter

Indian Churches and Indian Hymns in Southwestern Oklahoma

On a hot Sunday morning in mid-June 1998, Ralph Kotay and I drove to the J. J. Methvin Memorial United Methodist Church of Anadarko, Oklahoma—the Indian church named after the missionary John Jasper Methvin, who worked among the Kiowas from 1887 to 1908. We arrived in the church's parking lot with time to spare. Often Ralph and I took this time to talk about Kiowa hymns or to discuss the previous night's powwows, but this morning's heat drove us out of the car and into the air-conditioned church. Several other cars sat empty as well, attesting that the heat had perhaps driven more into the morning's Sunday school than usual.

Ralph and I walked through the back doors of the small church and made our way up the narrow hallway to the kitchen. There, seated around a small table, several of the older members were in an intense discussion about the morning's Bible reading from Job. They bid a brief hello to Ralph and me and continued their debate about witnessing to the unsaved. The smell of freshly brewed coffee immediately diverted my attention, however, and Ralph's as well. We both headed for the coffeepot, filled our cups, and then made our way into the sanctuary. We greeted and shook hands with friends and, with coffee cups in hand, settled into our normal spot near the back and close to the kitchen door. Here, we could have easy access to the coffeepot.

The small sanctuary was cool and inviting; sipping our hot coffee on this already sultry morning seemed a little less contradictory in here. Echoing the low-pitched hum of the air conditioner, the ceiling fans whirled at full speed. But the carpeted floor seemed to deaden the sound. More immediately audible were those entering the church. A dozen or so people slowly made their way into the sanctuary from both the kitchen and the church's main entryway. They shook hands and talked as they began taking their seats in the cushioned pews, two rows of which flanked the edges of the aisle leading to the front of the church. There, on a platform raised just a few feet above the floor, a sheet covered an altar with preparations for this month's Holy Communion. Above, firmly attached to the exact center of the wall, a large wooden cross spanning a few feet wide and several more high faced back to the incoming congregation. To its right and left, the American and United Methodist flags stood, respectively. A few feet on either side of the flags two modestly crafted and cushioned chairs sat empty. Two pulpits, one on each side of the stage, framed this arrangement. And on its outermost edges, a piano and organ rested, now silent.

The window's shades open, the sunlight danced across the soft white walls, which were adorned simply with a few wall hangings and pictures. A velvet image of Christ holding a lamb and leading a herd of sheep caught my eye this morning. I turned my attention back to the service's program, which Ralph and I each now had in hand and were reading. On its cover, below the words "bathed with tears," a color drawing depicted a water-filled bowl—its ringed ripples suggesting that it had been filled by droplets of tears. It rested atop a table, a towel at its base. A quick glance to the day's Bible readings written verbatim on the back of the program confirmed that the illustration referenced the day's gospel reading, Luke 7:36–50—the story of Jesus forgiving the sins of a woman who bathed his feet with her tears and dried them with her hair. Inside, I glanced over announcements, the monthly calendar, prayer requests, and the order of worship. With the exception of Holy Communion, the service was to proceed like most J. J. Methvin Sunday morning services. Following a musical prelude, a spoken welcome and prayer, and Sunday school report, the service would begin with a call to worship, recited from the program in unison. On this Sunday, the service would then turn to a hymn of praise from the gospel tradition, a hymn from the Methodist hymnal, and three Bible readings entitled "First Lesson," "Second Lesson," and "Gospel Reading." Next, the congregation would sing Native hymns, which at J. J. Methvin almost always meant Kiowa hymns (although at times Comanche hymns are sung as well). Following this singing, the church service would turn to the announcement of members' birthdays—which was often followed by the Kiowa birthday hymn—and "joys and concerns," which church members offered aloud to the rest of the congregation. Finally, after the pastoral prayer, tithes and offerings, and the musical doxology, the sermon on this day would preface Holy Communion. The final invocation, or benediction, would end the program.

By this time, J. J. Methvin's pastor, Robert Pinezaddleby, had risen, walked to the front of the sanctuary, and begun to greet all those in attendance. "I want to welcome you today," said Pinezaddleby after a while. "I believe we're ready for this morning's worship. As we prepare, we pray that the Holy Spirit will work with us, that the Holy Spirit will help us and *guide* us as we leave and as we go today." Several people continued visiting and talking as the service was slowly taking shape. Reverend Pinezaddleby turned toward the still dormant piano, silently acknowledging that the pianist had not yet arrived. The conventional musical prelude would not happen this Sunday. "We would like to have an opening hymn," Pinezaddleby said as a silence fell across the congregation. He looked over to where Ralph sat and motioned for him to start the song. Ralph took a deep breath, and on his exhale, the Kiowa words from the first stanza of the hymn resonated throughout the room (here translated into English):

If you are following the Jesus Road, be happy.

Several in the congregation joined in unison as Ralph progressed through the hymn's second, third, and fourth stanzas:

If you are following Jesus' way, be happy.
When you mention His name, He will give you salvation.
If you are following Jesus' way, there is joy.[1]

After singing the song through once, Ralph started it again. As we sang the song through three more times, I thought about why Ralph may have decided to sing this particular song; he always seemed to carefully choose the appropriate hymn for the occasion. With this in mind, I immediately thought back to what he had said the first time I heard him speak about this hymn in his weekly Kiowa hymn class: "The first time that the Indians began to get together, to worship in our modern-day churches that were brought way back in the 1800s—the Baptist churches, the Methodist churches—they sing this. It's an old, favorite song."

"These Songs Need to Go On"
A Meeting of Ralph Kotay's Kiowa Hymn Class

One evening in early January 1994 a small group gathered for Ralph's weekly hymn class in Anadarko, Oklahoma. Soon after those assembled sat down, Ralph spoke briefly about why he started his class on Kiowa Christian hymns. In the early 1990s, he had felt compelled to preserve a song tradition practiced by many of the Indian churches since before the turn of the twentieth century. Born in 1927, Ralph had grown up speaking the Kiowa language and singing traditional Kiowa hymns; now, fewer and fewer people were learning either the Kiowa language or the songs. "These songs need to go on," Ralph said as he started his class.

Ralph talked for a few moments about class logistics, then turned his attention back to hymns. "This first song I'll sing, it belongs to my uncle. He has a mind where that he's always thinking about the Almighty. I think that really helps him."

Many of those gathered — young and old alike — turned their recorders on, and Ralph sang the hymn. A few others joined in the singing.

When Ralph finished, he translated the hymn's words into English, then reflected on their broader meanings. "The words in that," he began, "it says: 'It is good that I have recognized You as my God. From here on I will be praying to You.' Then it repeats that same wording, over and over.

"You know," he continued, "if you're really a true believer, you're sincere about Christianity; these songs will somehow work with you. The words are *so* precious. The words get you to start thinking about your own life. That's the way *all* these songs are, no matter what tribe you're from. . . .

"[These Indian tribes] all have their different songs they like to sing. Say, for example, I sing around the drum, too." Ralph talked about his many years of powwow singing. "I've been around this singing *so* long," he said after a short while, "but *this* is the best type of singing that I do. I always praise, I always thank God for it, because I mention His name in every song; every time I'm in church, I mention His name. Sometimes I sing a song, it's for myself: how I've come through all the hardships, things like that — when my family gets sick. I pray to Him every day. And it makes you feel *good* to sing these songs. There are songs of thanksgiving, there are songs of sorrow, for people that are down and with sicknesses. We have songs of *all* kinds."

Ralph returned to the song he had sung just a few minutes before. "So this song says you have recognized Him as our God, *my* God: 'From here on I will pray to You.' That's what it has in that." [2]

"We Have Songs of *All* Kinds"
Singing Hymns in Southwestern Oklahoma

Throughout southwestern Oklahoma, Indian churches are today a significant part of Native American community life. The variety of

7. Ralph Kotay teaches his Kiowa hymn
class. Photo: Luke Eric Lassiter, 1994.

churches found here reflects the variety that one would find in most any American community. But while Indian churches share basic doctrine with their denominational counterparts in other American communities, their obvious differences in membership, individual church histories, and the use of tribal language in speech and song have brought about a unique Christian practice that situates these Indian churches specifically within an American Indian experience.

In southwestern Oklahoma, where Ralph Kotay lives and teaches his hymn class, Indian churches serve a diverse Native population, including Kiowa, Kiowa-Apache, Chiricahua Apache, Caddo, Wichita, Comanche, and Delaware peoples.[3] While several of these churches have intertribal memberships (and include non-Indians), many churches have tribal-specific memberships and may serve primarily Kiowa or Comanche or Caddo congregations. In these congregations—and to a certain extent in those with intertribal congregations—the singing of traditional Indian hymns is an important component of each service.

Indian hymns are only one kind of song sung at these Indian churches, however. They share their place in any given service with English hymns (sung from hymnals) and, in some churches, gospel song. While hymnal songs and those that spring from a gospel tradition are most often sung in English, Indian hymns are almost always rendered in a specific tribal language. Indian hymns not only differ from English hymns and gospel in language and content; they also differ in their performance as well. English hymns are frequently sung from hymnals, accompanied by a piano or organ, and often sung while standing; gospel is sometimes sung from sheet music, may include guitars and microphones, and is usually performed at the front of the church, but Indian hymns generally have no accompaniment (except in some Pentecostal churches, where a small drum is sometimes used), are most often sung while seated, and are recalled completely from memory.[4]

When Indian hymns are called for in a service, either from the written program or spontaneously, an individual "starts" the song. That individual is usually a man, but women sometimes start songs, too. After the first several words of the song's first stanza are sung through aloud and congregants have ascertained what song the individual is singing—for many songs have similar "starts"—those who know the song join in unison.

When the congregation completes the song once, the song's starter either repeats all or part of the hymn anew (depending on the hymn's form), and the song is sung through in unison again.[5] The hymn is usually sung through two to four times, with the song's starter ending the song simply by not starting it again. After a hymn is completed, the same (or another) individual might lead another song if one is called for, or if the Spirit is moving the service.

A singer working within most Indian hymn traditions has an enormous range of possibilities from which to choose a song. As Ralph Kotay says above, speaking of Kiowa hymns: "We have songs of *all* kinds." But a singer does not necessarily choose songs at random. Singers like Ralph, being led by the Spirit of the service, often carefully select the appropriate hymn for the appropriate occasion. "The words that are put in there [in these hymns]," says Ralph, "they're for every occasion. . . . There's a song for everything."[6] From baptismal hymns to funeral, prayer, and even birthday hymns, this wide range of songs thus engages a wide range of purposes, helping to clarify and deepen the sentiments associated with any given moment within any given church service.

Generally, Indian hymns in southwestern Oklahoma's Indian community—in sound, structure, performance, and use—are not entirely unlike many other Indian hymn traditions.[7] But with regard to meaning, Indian hymns are situated within very particular tribal traditions. Hymns belong to larger tribal song repertoires as much as they belong to Christian song repertoires. "Every tribe that we have," says Ralph, "they have their own songs."[8] In this way, hymns simultaneously communicate a combination of Christian and tribal-specific experience—pointing us to a deep level of experiential encounter that reaches beyond discrete musicological categories such as musical sound, structure, performance, and use.

"The Words Are *So* Precious"
On Language and Story

But just what do Indian hymns communicate about this experiential encounter? The unique and complex intersection between Christianity, specific tribal histories, and individuals is clarified by the "language of hymns," which includes both what the language *in* song explicitly relates and communicates as well as the language *surrounding* song—that is, the voiced stories and sentiments that hymns invoke. Taken together, the language in and surrounding song provides an important window into the deeper meanings of Indian hymns in southwestern Oklahoma. Consider, for example, the following Kiowa hymn (here translated into English line by line):

> It is good that God made my spirit feel good. I am glad.
> It is Him: He is the One who made my spirit feel good. I am glad.
> It is good that God made my spirit feel good.
> One day, I felt so bad and so lonely.
> It is good that God made my spirit feel good.
>
> It is Him: He is the One who made my spirit feel good. I am glad.
> It is good that God made my spirit feel good.
> One day, I felt so bad and so lonely.
> It is good that God made my spirit feel good.[9]

The words in this song obviously communicate a positive experience in which God turned sadness into joy. But this song, as sung in the communicative context of knowledgeable listeners, also references more than this. Ralph says of the hymn, "I heard this [song] a *long* time ago. My uncle, he's a good singer. He's made some songs. . . . This one particular song, he was telling me — 'You know, nephew, when I was young, I went to church. And I also went to the Native American Church. We *all* pray about the same thing, about something in our lives. This one time, this particular time, my wife had gone away. God had taken her away. I was really depressed. I was sitting there in the room by myself and thinking about things in my life. Later on, this song came to me. It came to me through the gladness of my heart. I'm glad I sung [it] because it seemed to lift all that depression off of me.' " [10]

While the language in this hymn generally communicates a relationship between God and an individual, the language surrounding this song extends the relationship further and situates it between Ralph and his uncle, and between Ralph's uncle and God. But that which this song references is not limited to Ralph's story. This (and every) song summons many layers of spoken interpretations, narratives, and individual sentiments. All of this is to say, therefore, that a song's meaning is not entirely defined by the words in the song; the words are the symbolic foundation on which broader narrative meanings are built.

Given this, Ralph and others explain that there is much more to the significance and meaning of hymns in their community, especially in regard to the significance of language itself. In southwestern Oklahoma, fewer and fewer people use Native languages in everyday conversation, but Native language continues to command a central place in public events. While most every single person who gathers at any given powwow, peyote meeting, or church service speaks English, Native language emerges not just in song but also in prayer and oral presentations. Obviously, language has a communicative role at these events; many elders, for example, say that some things just cannot be spoken (or sung) in English like they can "in Indian." But Native language fulfills much more than its obvious communicative role, especially because most everyone gathered at any given event may not fully understand the Native language being publicly vocalized. The use of Native language also communicates a connection to that which came before, that which is traditional, and, for many, that which is godly. Many elders say they pray in their Native language because it is the language that God gave to them specifically and uniquely. "Father, we consider that You have given everything that we see, and have done everything for us that is good," prays one individual in English at a powwow before praying in his Native language. "You have given us our language, dear Father, and this great gift of music." [11]

The language in hymns, then, provides not only referents for individual stories; for many people—especially but not limited to elders —the sung performance of tribal language in hymns also enacts a larger, shared community experience with God and Christianity and an experiential relationship echoed in many songs. Expressions in song such as "God made my spirit feel good" are regularly heard in Kiowa hymns, but they are not as ambiguous as they sound. For many Kiowa singers and listeners, for example, this seemingly vague sentiment actually emerges from a very particular manifestation of God's presence in the lives of a very specific people. "If you *understand* the *real* meaning, the *deep* meaning—that's what makes these songs so beautiful," says Ralph. "When this Christianity came into our area, they [Kiowas] were so dedicated to this Christianity that these songs [came to them]. They don't compose these songs. They come to them through the Spirit. That's the reason why they're so beautiful. *All* these songs." [12] For those like Ralph, the "deep meaning" of hymns is that which simultaneously encompasses and transcends the multiplicity of individual interpretations, stories, and specific histories of individual songs: a long-established relationship with God as expressed and felt in song, a felt encounter that Ralph and others express in English as "Spirit."

"And It Makes You Feel *Good* to Sing These Songs"
On the Relationship of Spirit to Kiowa Hymns

When talking about hymns in southwestern Oklahoma's Indian community, Spirit implies a godly encounter with song that occurs in the context of a Christian experience. This Christian experience, however, is a relatively recent addition to a broader narrative of encounter with the godly; in community-wide conversations, talk about Spirit denotes a godly encounter with all song — not just hymns — and it precedes the institution of Christianity in the community.[13] "Anytime we sing a song on His behalf," says Ralph, reflecting on the relationship between all Kiowa song and God, "we mention God, Daw-kee. That's always the way it's been, even before the missionaries came. . . . The Kiowa religious songs that we have, those songs that were sung, even before the missionaries came, all the songs pertain to God — the words are in there."[14]

While the Kiowa word Daw-kee now denotes in English "God," importantly, the root for both Daw-kee and the Kiowa word for song, *daw-gyah,* is *daw,* "power"; *daw* was and is that which materializes in song as Spirit.[15] Those like Ralph say that Kiowa song affirms a relationship that was established long ago in time immemorial, when the first Kiowa song was sung. Today, almost all Kiowa song — from peyote to powwow — maintains this relationship with the godly. Thus, Kiowa singers, whether singing hymns or peyote songs, further this relationship through singing, but God also reciprocates by continually giving songs to Kiowa people. As Ralph states above, "They don't compose these songs. They come to them through the Spirit."[16] Understood in this light, song itself is an unfolding testimony of a long-established relationship between Daw-kee and Kiowa people, individually expressed to those like Ralph's uncle but made relevant to a larger community of believers through the act of singing.

Kiowa hymns obviously express a unique Christian component of this unfolding and ongoing relationship. "Everything that we sing in our Kiowa hymns now," says Ralph, "modern-day songs, it's always mentioned about Daw-kee. When the missionaries came, that's where we learned about Jesus, the Son of God. He's the one that God created—Him, just like we are now, when He walked the earth. He was called the Son of God, Jesus."[17] While the language in song engages a long-established relationship between Kiowa people and the godly, the language surrounding hymns—whether stories told in English or testimonies delivered in Kiowa—help to clarify the emergence of a unique Christian practice in the community since before the turn of the twentieth century.

"These Songs Need to Go On"
On Maintaining and Preserving a Godly Relationship

Language, story, and song are thus at the heart of maintaining a specific connection to the godly that is generations old but that continues to materialize in the here and now. At church services, this godly connection emerges in prayer, testimony, and song—deepening the ever-emerging story about God, Indian people, and Christianity. "I feel like our forefathers—our grandmothers and them—they prayed a lot," says Anita Blackbear at one of Ralph's hymn classes. "And they were with the Lord a lot. We don't do that today. And I don't feel like we've composed songs like that. But *they* really were believers in the Holy Spirit. I feel like that's *why* they were given these songs. For us."[18]

While language, story, and song sharpen a connection to the past, to tribal memory, and to God, these expressions also provide the foundation for building the future of this relationship. For many like Ralph, some of the most meaningful components of this godly connection are threatened. "We don't have that many song leaders anymore," says Ralph to his Kiowa hymn class. "Our young men, they don't seem to care [about being song leaders in the churches]. Even our language, a lot of us don't understand. . . . In our time, we're just too busy. We're all young and we don't care to learn these words [of the hymns]. That's where we're at [today]."[19]

Ralph's sentiments do not just represent an older generation bemoaning the passing of "old times." On the contrary, those like Ralph acknowledge that maintaining Kiowa language, story, and song not only means the continuance of a particular way of understanding and articulating experience; it also means maintaining a specific and precious relationship with God. Ralph's hymn class, then, is about preserving not only song or language or story but also that which these expressions sustain: a unique American Indian Christian practice in southwestern Oklahoma.

Ralph Kotay, edited by Ralph Kotay and Luke Eric Lassiter

Kiowa Hymns and Their Deeper Meanings

Commentary on the Field Recordings (Compact Disc)

There is an old Kiowa hymn that makes the following expression: "God, You have created the earth. You have created life. You have permitted me to enjoy this creation, this life. You have permitted me to live. And I always feel good because of that." This song, like many songs, causes us to think about our lives. When you wake up in the morning, you see daylight. And you thank God that He has given you another day to see and enjoy all His creation. When you stop and look, everything is so beautiful.

Every day, I think just like this, no matter what day it is. Because God permits me to see another day. And I feel good about it. In this way, I sit down and pray about everybody's life. Because sometimes, some families have sickness and illness among them, even death. We don't know our futures. But then, He does. And so, I pray for their lives. *That's* what I really enjoy about life now.

I'm over seventy years old, and it seems like my life has really changed since I went through a terrible sickness several years ago. I went through something that was really terrible and I had a serious surgery. My mom, when she passed away, she had the same kind of sickness that I had. So the night before I went into surgery, I was really thinking about all the responsibilities I had. My wife, my children, my grandchildren: How are they going to be if I leave? But while I lay there waiting for my surgery, many people came into my hospital room and prayed for my life. They prayed for me, and that encouraged me. And I told the Lord then if He would let me live I would do my best to continue His work. "Do with me what You will," I said.

Yes, there is power in prayer. I know this is true, because I came through okay; and today, I'm with you. After the surgery, it seemed like I just wanted to do more for God. Because He permitted me to stay on this earth for a little while longer.

After getting out of the hospital, I went to a church meeting to thank God and to thank those who had prayed for me. My brother stood up to speak. "Ralph, God has a purpose for you," he said. "That's why you're here. He still has some work for you to do. He extended your life a little longer so you can teach these songs."

SELECTION 1

Ralph Kotay and Pearl Kotay, southwestern Oklahoma, c. 1965, recording by Raymond Weryavah

I was born in Apache, Oklahoma, on 7 September 1927. There I was born and raised by my parents, Ray and Pearl Kotay. They raised me in a Christian home. And because I grew up as a Christian, I heard these Kiowa hymns my whole life. My dad, he was a song leader. And Mom knew a lot of these songs, too. As I was growing up, they took me to church and Dad would sing these church hymns there. And of course, when we were at home, when we were sitting around the house, we would sing these songs. Mom, when she was cooking, she would be singing these hymns. All that time, those songs were going into my mind, songs that came from the early churches — like Saddle Mountain, Rainy Mountain, and Elk Creek. Of course, if you're in that kind of environment and you're in that frame of mind, and you like to sing — well, naturally, you're going to pick up songs. So that's the way it was with me.

In this first song, Mom and I are singing an old song from one of those old churches. It says,

If you are following the Jesus Road, be happy.
If you are following Jesus' way, be happy.
When you mention His name, He will give you salvation.
If you are following Jesus' way, there is joy.[1]

There's a lot of meanings to these songs. The words affect a person in different ways. If you know the words to these songs, if you *really* know, the words apply to your life. Like for our Kiowa people, following the Christian way is very serious; whenever they turn their ways into a good way, such as going to church, their lives seem to change for the good. For those who have gone along this road, the words, then, take on deep meanings. That's what makes these songs *so* beautiful. And this is what this song is about. If you are following God's way, He will make you happy.

SELECTIONS 2–3

A "Singing" at the J. J. Methvin Memorial United Methodist Church, Ralph Kotay and his Kiowa hymn class, February 1994

This song is my mother's song:[2]

[Selection 2]

We have come to the house of the Lord to be saved.
We have come to the house of the Lord to be saved.
God has given us His son.
God has given us His son for our salvation.
Let us all pray; it is the only truthful way.

It came to my mother many years ago when she was just a young woman, long before I was born. When I was a boy, playing around the house, she stopped me and told me about it. She said, "Son, this song came to me through the Spirit of God." She told me about when she was a child, she always went to church with her parents at Saddle Mountain Indian Baptist Church. And this was in her mind when this song came to her. She thought about her life, and when this song came, everything was there in this song—all of her thoughts.

That's the way our Kiowa hymns come. My father, he also had a song come to him (like my mother, it happened when he was young). It was the same way with my grandmother and grandfather. Many of our Christian people have had songs come to them in this way. Especially the old people—like my dad and mom and their parents—they believed so strongly in those days, in such a way that these songs just came to them according to how they thought about their lives as Christians. This has always been our way since Christianity came into our area way back in the 1800s and early 1900s. The old people were so sincere; they believed in God so much that these songs just came to them. Since then, we've had a lot of people who have made songs.

Many times we say that a song was "made" or "composed" by a particular person. But these songs are not composed, actually. They come through the Spirit and the minds of the people who really believe. While many of our hymns are so old that we don't know who made them anymore, every single song goes back to how a particular individual felt when the song came to them: they had a feeling that they wanted to express. Like this song:

[Selection 3]

> *The Spirit of God: He knows. He is the One who will make you feel good. He is the One who knows.*
> *The Spirit of God, He is the One.*
> *He is the One who will make you feel good.*
> *He knows.*
> *He knows.*
> *He knows.*
> *The Spirit of God: He knows. He is the One who will make you feel good. He is the One who knows.*

The Spirit of God, He is the One.
He is the One who will make you feel good.
He knows.
He knows.
He knows.
The Spirit of God: He knows. He is the One who will make you feel
good. He is the One who knows.

I don't know who made this hymn, but I sing it about any time at church
services. Sometimes I sing it when people are depressed, sick, or feeling
down—like at a funeral. At other times, it can go the other way. When
we're having thanksgiving services, this song is appropriate. Either way,
God knows what you're thinking about and He'll make you feel good—
whether you're going through thanksgiving or hardship.

SELECTION 4

Ralph Kotay and his Kiowa hymn class, April 1994

Sometimes I sing this hymn as an invitation song during revivals:[3]

Jesus is calling us to be saved.
Let us all pray to Him.
Jesus is calling us to be saved.
Let us all be happy.
Jesus, Jesus: God's way is good.
Jesus is calling us to be saved.
Let us all be happy.

This particular song is sung with a tune from an English hymn, but
the Kiowa words were put in the song by an individual, just like my
mother's song. There are very few Kiowa hymns like this. Most of the
songs that we consider Kiowa hymns are original songs "made" by
Kiowa people.

These Kiowa songs are not written down like English hymns. We sing them from memory; we've kept them close to our minds and in our hearts since the very first time they were made. That's why they're so beautiful to us. When our elders first came out with these songs many years ago, they sung them in such a way that when you hear it—if you understand the language—you can take the song into yourself. Just like me, I hear and sing these songs, and I can take a song into myself—like this one—and say, I am thankful and happy that Jesus called me and made a way for me.

SELECTIONS 5–7

A "singing" at the J. J. Methvin Memorial United Methodist Church, Ralph Kotay and his Kiowa hymn class, May 1994

Another song that we sing with an English tune is "Amazing Grace," but here again, our Kiowa words are different than in the English version:

[Selection 5]

> *God, He is going to save us.*
> *Let us all come, let us all come and worship.*
> *Because God, He is going to save us.*
> *Let us all come, let us all come and worship.*

This is an old hymn, of course, and we often use it as an invitational song at church services—with or without a piano. The Kiowa words used here are the original words. There is a different, newer Kiowa version of this same song sung to the tune of "Amazing Grace." And sometimes there's confusion over which version to sing, but a few of our hymns are like this. Some song leaders or church congregations may change a hymn's words slightly from the original, and so a particular hymn may be sung different from one church to the next. Choirs, for example, have sometimes changed the words in the Kiowa version of "Amazing Grace" to better fit with that type of singing.

8. Ralph's Kiowa hymn class gathers at
J. J. Methvin Memorial United Method-
ist Church for a singing. Pictures (*left
to right*): Trina Stumblingbear, Mildred
Kotay, Stephanie Starr, and Theresa
Carter. Photo: Luke Eric Lassiter, 1994.

Words are not the only thing that people have changed in some of these hymns. Some song leaders and churches choose to sing the hymns faster now. Some of them even use a small hand drum; they beat it to the hymn's rhythm while they're singing. But when it comes to *me* personally and how *I* choose to sing, I always sing the hymns the original way, the way I was taught by my parents from the time I was a child. When you sing these songs the old way, you get a lot out of these songs; you get that original meaning. To me, the original words to "Amazing Grace" are just like this; people at that time were true believers and these are their original expressions received through the Spirit.

At church services, we do sing songs from hymnals just like at any other church. Most of these, of course, are sung in English. But a very few are written and sung in Kiowa. Like this one, from the *United Methodist Hymnal,* hymn number 330:

[Selection 6]

> *God, I am praying to you.*
> *God, I am praying to you.*
> *Hear me, for I am tired; I am praying to you.*
> *Come and be with me.*[4]

This song was made recently within the last several years. The way that this song *sounds* with the English tune — this is like the very first hymns that the missionaries taught us. But even before the missionaries came, our people already knew God; we were a praying people already. And we prayed to the Creator. The missionaries, they brought in what the old Indians used to call the "Jesus Road." They brought us the Bible. And they brought us their songs with the English tunes, but they really didn't catch on. We had our own way of singing. Actually, our Kiowa hymns are very similar to our Ghost Dance songs from way back. It's really surprising, but many of those Ghost Dance songs say almost the same thing as the Bible. Many white people back then in the 1800s, they thought the Ghost Dance was going to lead to an Indian uprising. But those Indians were praying to meet their relatives in heaven—just like Christians. And their Ghost Dance songs, they came to the people in the same way that our Kiowa hymns come today. All of our traditional Kiowa songs are like this really. Native American Church songs, pow-wow songs, hymns—many of them come in the same way, from God, through His Spirit.

So, when the missionaries came out here, they began to teach us the Bible. The ones like Isabel Crawford would teach us through interpreters—like Lucius Aitsan—who would tell us what the missionary was saying. But again, the people already had such a strong belief in God that when they turned their thoughts toward the Jesus Road, they hoped that some day after they left the earth that they would see their loved ones again in heaven. And this is where the songs came in. They believed in such a way that these songs would just come to them. There were a few songs that had an English tune, which they would put their own words in, like the ones we sing now from time to time. But the ones that were brought out by the Indians, those songs came to them according to what they thought in their minds—through knowing the Spirit of God. Like once, when this old Kiowa man heard about how Jesus had been crucified, he thought about it a long time, and then all of a sudden a song came to him: an old song that we still sing today from the very beginning of our Christianity. Songs like these we've been singing over and over ever since that time.

We say, then, that these church hymns are something that God gave us, to us as Kiowas. Today, we enjoy these songs day after day. And every day, these songs make us think about our lives. Like the following song, which I first heard many, many years ago at the Saddle Mountain Indian Baptist Church, a song that my dad used to sing:

[Selection 7]

> *Jesus, I am going to pray to you. Forgive me.*
> *Jesus, I am going to pray to you. Forgive me.*
> *Jesus, my thoughts are not right. Forgive me.*

This song is meant to express the thoughts that the elders often had when they prayed. They were *so sincere;* they were very humble people. Before they prayed, they would sit for a long time and think. But sometimes they would cry, because their thoughts were not right. This is what this song is about. If I'm not mistaken, I think it was made by Delos Lonewolf in the early 1900s.

SELECTIONS 8–10

Ralph Kotay and his Kiowa hymn class, December 1993

In 1993, I started teaching a Kiowa hymn class. Since then, we've met mainly during the fall, winter, and spring months—the summer's just too hot. In the beginning, when I first started this class, we had just a few turn out. But as time went along, more and more people started showing up. And today, I'm still teaching my hymn class when I can.

We had never had a class like this, but I just happened to mention it one day. I said I wanted to teach the younger folks so that maybe one day they could come in at these prayer services that we have, these Sunday services that we have, and sing these songs. I wanted the younger people to come to church and start taking up this Christianity, and taking up these traditional songs that we have. I wanted to have a lot of young men, especially—because they are supposed to start the songs. I know many of them have the ability because many have begun to start songs around the powwow drum, and that's good—because God gave us these things, everything that we have. That's the way it's been ever since we were born and came into existence.

So, after I mentioned one day that I wanted to teach a hymn class, I decided that I should do it, because God allowed me to live so I could teach these songs. He's got work for me. He's given me a voice; He's given me something to sing about; He's given me something to help others with. And for that, I give thanks to Him every day. I love teaching my class, because I praise Him with every song that I sing.

When I started planning to teach my class, then, I told the people that regardless of who they are, they would be welcome in my class. I'll teach anybody, I said. Some of our song leaders, they don't want to teach the songs; they say, "I don't want to teach you those things. Those are our songs." I say that these are God's songs and that they belong to every-body. These songs have been handed down, and today, I'm glad that they are here with us. But some day, all of this might be gone. It doesn't have to be; it *can* go on and on if we want it to. That's why I decided I *had* to teach my class. That's why I'm trying to pass on these songs to our children and our grandchildren as they grow up.

Ever since I started the class, many of my students have come week after week to hear my singing. I teach the beginners easy songs at first so they can pick them up. Songs like this:

[Selection 8]

> *Thank you God, You have helped me.*
> *Thank you God, You have helped me.*
> *I prayed to You, and You helped me.*
> *I prayed to You, and You helped me.*
> *I was depressed.*
> *And You helped me.*
> *I am glad.*

This is the first song that children usually learn in our churches. The words are simple and it's easy to pick up. When I'm teaching our younger people to sing a song like this, I tell them to go ahead and start the song at church when the opportunity arises. Now, I tell them the first time that they sing it, they'll probably be nervous, because they'll be afraid that they might mess up or sing the words wrong. But I tell them that the people who are really sincere about going to church won't make fun of them or criticize them because they know you're trying. Church people will only encourage you.

At each class that I teach, the people bring their recorders. I sing the songs and explain the words, what type of song it is, and what it's for. I do this because we have so many songs for so many purposes, songs for all different occasions and for all the different types of services that we have. We have songs for thanksgiving, for baptism, for birthdays, for sorrow, for a loss in the family—for everything. Like this Easter song that we often sing at Easter services or at other times when it's appropriate:

[Selection 9]

> It was Jesus who hung on the cross.
> It was Jesus who hung on the cross.
> Let us pray to Him.
> Let us pray to Him.
> The people were lost in sin.
> They hung Him on the cross.
>
> Let us pray to Him.
> Let us pray to Him.
> The people were lost in sin.
> They hung Him on the cross.

I learned this song from my parents. My mom told me about how they used to sing this song at Saddle Mountain Indian Baptist Church. There was an old man there, Old Man Gotebo they called him. He loved to sing this hymn. And each time he sang it, he kept time with the song by hitting the floor with this cane. My mother said it was a sight to see, almost comical.

Many times, I tell my students stories like this so they can understand the history and the people behind the songs. And of course, many of the people who attend my classes are church people, and they have lots of stories, too. So much of the time we end up talking about the songs together and what they mean to us. And because of this, we end up talking about how these songs make us feel, how uplifting they are, and how God will help us with the problems that we have when we call upon Him—just like this song so beautifully expresses:

[Selection 10]

> *We have come here to worship Jesus.*
> *We have come here to worship Jesus.*
> *We have come with mixed emotions.*
> *God, come closer and help us with the problems that we have.*

This is a very special song to me. My late wife, my dearest companion Mildred, loved this song. Sometimes, her feelings were just like what the words say, and she would ask me to sing this song. Or if someone had a loss in their family or they were hurting somehow, she would ask me to sing this song as a prayer. She would pray that God would come closer to them and help them with the problems they had. That's the way Mildred was. We were married for fifty-two years and I never heard her say a bad thing about anyone. She was the perfect Christian; she always wanted the best for people. She just loved everybody. And this song is meant for everyone just in that way. Yes, I could sing this song all day long.

SELECTIONS 11–18

Ralph Kotay with Pat Kopepasah and Letha Peters, December 2000

In many of these songs, even though you have near about the same words, they each have different meanings. That's because on each song, the thoughts are different; and the stories are different. Yes, I always say that the thoughts that go behind these songs are very sincere. We know this to be true for every song that we sing. But, as I've said before, when you hear a song, all you are hearing are the words. If you understand what the words *mean*—the thoughts and stories behind them—they have deeper meanings. Take, for example, this song:

9. Letha Peters (*left*), Ralph Kotay (*center*),
and Pat Kopepasah (*right*) record Kiowa
hymns. Photo: Elizabeth Campbell, 2000.

[Selection 11]

How happy I am that God made a way for me. My spirit is happy.
Jesus made a way for me.
How happy I am that God made a way for me.
My spirit is happy.
My spirit is happy.
How happy I am; my spirit is happy.

Jesus made a way for me.
How happy I am that God made a way for me.
My spirit is happy.
My spirit is happy.
How happy I am; my spirit is happy.

The person who made this hymn had a certain feeling that they wanted to share. Their thoughts were in such a way that they wanted people to understand what the Lord has done for them. It's just like my cousin's song:

[Selection 12]

It is good that God has shown me the way. Through the Holy Spirit He has shown me the way. It is good that He has made my heart feel good.
I didn't know.
I hesitated to go to Him. But I am glad that He has come to be with me. He has come to be with me in Spirit.
Today, I am glad.
He has shown me the way. I always feel good now. I am always glad.

I didn't know.
I hesitated to go to Him. But I am glad that He has come to be with me. He has come to be with me in Spirit.
Today, I am glad.
He has shown me the way. I always feel good now. I am always glad.

This song applies to so many people who come to follow the Jesus Road. It was made by Percy Anquoe. He's my brother; because he's my dad's sister's son, I call him my "brother," Kiowa way. He had a wild life in his younger years. And all that time, his wife was going to church and taking the kids there. But he wasn't going to church. One day, he said, he slowly started going. And after a while, he was saved, saved from the bad things he was doing. He said that soon after that, he was out at the wood pile, chopping wood. He said he was just sitting there thinking, and a feeling came over him. He began to pray. And pretty soon, this song came to him. As it did, he cried.

Percy brought this song to church and testified about how the song came. "I was thinking about my life when this song came to me," he said. Well, Dad was living at that time, and he said, "My son [he called him son because Percy was his own nephew], you've really made a good service for us today. Because you've truly changed your life over to Christianity." After that, Percy became a deacon in the church, taught Sunday school, and became very active in this way of life. He did a lot of good things.

The words in this song just fit my brother's life perfectly. They fit my life, too; I was a lot like him at different points in my life. I too took life for granted. I had my fun. Of course, many of us are like this. In our earlier lives, we're careless. We don't care much about going to church, even though we have the chance to. But we just don't, because as kids, we have our own things to do. As we grow up as young men and women, we often start doing things wrong, like drinking, partying, and all that. Percy made this song with this in his mind. And that's why I really love it. It applies to so many of us. So often, then, I think to myself: if our young people understood the words of this song, it would fit them.

I have spoken about this song many times to many people. I tell them about it because the song and its story are a testimony to how this Christian way of life is. It just seems like you want to do good when you hear these songs; it just seems like you want to pray to the Lord even more. And it makes you so glad and happy. This is what this next song is about:

[Selection 13]

I prayed to God and He made my heart glad. And I am glad.
I prayed to God and He made my heart glad.
I am glad.
I am glad.
I am glad.
I prayed to God and He made my heart glad. And I am glad.

I prayed to God and He made my heart glad.
I am glad.
I am glad.
I am glad.
I prayed to God and He made my heart glad. And I am glad.

This song was made by Rev. George Kauyedouauty. Although the words are simple, they are expressing that feeling of joy, the feeling of being on this Jesus Road. When you're in that Spirit, you just want to praise Him. These are the kinds of songs that our elders like to hear; as I said, they really believe, and because they do, these songs often hit them in a certain way. It makes them feel good. And sometimes the songs even make them cry, because the words apply to their lives in so many different ways.

This song is the same way:

[Selection 14]

What Jesus does for you is so amazing!
What Jesus does for you is so amazing!
He does for you. And if you think about it and believe, it is amazing.
So be happy.
So be happy.
Up in heaven with Jesus, everything is so amazing.
There is a life in heaven that is amazing.

There is a word in this song that expresses the overwhelming feeling of recognizing God and the things He has done for you. That word is *gyah-som-me*. Roughly, it means "amazing." That's the closest way I can translate it. But when you're singing it, you know what that feeling is. If you understand what that word means, then it really is something else! See, everything that the living God does, it's amazing when you sit down and really think about it. This is what this song is saying.

Here is an old song, one of the oldest that we have:

[Selection 15]

> *God, do you want me to work for You?*
> *God, do you want me to work for You?*
> *If you want me to work for You, come and be with me.*
> *If you want me to work for You, take away my sins.*
> *But God, if You call me, I am ready to go to paradise.*
> *But God, if You call me, I am ready to go to paradise.*

We don't sing this hymn much anymore. Every once in a while, someone will sing it. If a person is really sick, or if they have done something wrong and they want to repent their sins, we might sing this song so that the Almighty might come and be with them and get them well.

This song was made by Rev. Sherman Chaddlesone. He was one of our first ministers at the Saddle Mountain Indian Baptist Church. I have heard that the song came to him when he was sick. He didn't know if he would live or die. And so he prayed that if God wanted him to continue preaching the Word, he would with His help. But, Sherman said, if God wanted to take him, he was ready.

Here is another song that our elders like to hear, especially when they've had a loss in their family. We often sing it at funerals so that people can remain strong in the faith.

[Selection 16]

> *God, come closer and be with us.*
> *God, come closer and be with us.*
> *Be with us during our loss that we have in our family.*
> *And because of You, our thoughts will help us overcome this.*

Songs like this remind us of how hard it is to live this life. It's especially hard when you've lost a loved one. But in the Bible, God reminds us that He is with us always, regardless of what problems we go through. Many songs relate to this, but this song in particular says it very directly:

[Selection 17]

> *God, this is your word.*
> *God, this is your word.*
> *Your word says that You will help me.*
> *Your word says that You will help me.*
> *God, You said that You will be with me.*
> *You said that You will help me with these hard times.*
> *God, You said that You will be with me.*

We often sing this song at funerals, too. It makes the people feel good to know that God is with them and helping them through their hard times. People's emotions can be so mixed at such times. Their minds are not clear. So that's why I sing songs like this. It puts their thoughts at ease, especially for those who really believe in this Christian way. For those who have praised the Lord their whole lives, it comforts them to know that God said these things, that He has left us His Word, His promise. For believers who understand the song's words, then, it makes them feel good.

I have a cousin—a brother—who was once a great song leader among our Kiowa people. But it wasn't always that way. One day he lost his son and they had a wake service for the boy. I was there and helped sing that night. I sang all kinds of songs that fit into that service, songs that were appropriate to this specific occasion. The words touched my brother in such a way and it made him feel so good that he decided to start singing Kiowa hymns right then and there. And after that, he became a well-known song leader. Many people asked him to sing at all kinds of services, including our funerals.

See, singing these hymns is such a serious part of our lives, from beginning to end. We live in a very close community, and funerals are also a major part of our lives. It seems that whenever someone dies, we're all affected, and we all try to go and support the family in their time of loss. I go to funerals a lot because I'm asked to sing often. Of course, I'm really glad to do this; I want to do my part to comfort the family. Singing hymns allows me to do something for them in my own way, to touch the family with this Word of God. It really makes *me* feel good to do this, and to tell the people about His Word—just like this song expresses.

[Selection 18]

> *You have heard the word of God.*
> *You have heard the word of God.*
> *All you people, all you people, praise Him!*
> *I prayed.*
> *I prayed.*
> *Look at me: I worshiped Him and He saved me.*
> *I prayed.*
> *And he saved me.*

SELECTIONS 19–20

Ralph Kotay with Luke Eric Lassiter and Pat Kopepasah, recorded by KRPT Radio for *Indians for Indians*, December 1998

Here is a song that I really like to sing:[5]

[Selection 19]

> *Thank You God.*
> *Thank You God that You are with me.*
> *Thank You God for showing me the way.*
> *Also, Jesus, You have shown me the way to heaven.*
> *So I want to thank You God that You are always with me.*
> *We are here just for a short while; thank you God for showing me*
> the way.

And here is another:

[Selection 20]

> *Who is He who has come to save us?*
> *Who is He who has come to save us?*
> *It was Jesus who came to save us.*
> *Why did Jesus come to save us?*
> *For all mankind, He has come to save us.*
>
> *Why did Jesus come to save us?*
> *For all mankind, He has come to save us.*

In both of these songs, you can hear the English word "Jesus." In our hymns, we use this word as well as our own Kiowa word for the Son of God. Daw-kee is God in the Kiowa language and Daw-gyah-ee means "Son of God." But of course, Jesus, Daw-kee, and Daw-gyah-ee all have about the same meaning; they each refer to the Almighty.

SELECTIONS 21–22

Ralph Kotay and his Kiowa hymn class, January 1994

Here are two more songs that I really like to sing. This first one was made by my uncle, Francis Tsonetokoy.

[Selection 21]

> *Who has given us life? It is Jesus who has given us life.*
> *He is the One who has given us life.*
> *It is Jesus who has given us life.*
> *It is good that He has given us life.*
> *So you must pray to Him.*
>
> *He is the One who has given us life.*
> *It is Jesus who has given us life.*
> *It is good that He has given us life.*
> *So you must pray to Him.*

And this second one was made by my aunt, Louise Doyebi Satie Tsatigh.

[Selection 22]

> *God has opened the heavenly doors for me.*
> *God has opened the heavenly doors for me.*
> *And I am glad.*
> *He has called me, and I am glad.*
> *My children, always pray.*
> *My children, always pray and worship.*
> *I'll meet you in heaven.*
> *God is the One who saves.*
> *My children, always pray and worship.*
> *I'll meet you in heaven.*

This second song came to my aunt a very long time ago. Just like all other songs, it came through the Spirit. She was such a strong believer.

Here again, my aunt's song is another that's very appropriate for a funeral. With this hymn, we honor someone. The person that's gone— it might be a grandmother, a grandfather, a mother, or a father—if they were someone who worshiped their whole life, we honor them by singing this song. And we try to encourage the children through these words, to encourage them to keep on praying—because we want to remind them that they will meet their parent or grandparent again. You know, it just seems like this song uplifts them; it makes them feel good because they think about what the deceased did for them. In our mind and in our thoughts, we want them to understand that this is what the deceased is trying to tell them: that someday I will meet you again in heaven.

SELECTIONS 23–25

Ralph Kotay, June 2000

There are three more songs that I wanted to make sure were on this recording. And I've added them here.

The first two songs are baptism songs. The first of these is the Methodist baptism hymn.

[Selection 23]

> *God, look at us.*
> *God, look at us.*
> *This water of life.*
> *We place it on our head.*
> *God, look at us.*
> *God, look at us.*
> *Also, Your Son Jesus, He is the One watching over us.*
> *Let us come.*
> *We will all be saved.*

And the second is the Baptist baptism hymn, but it has a different sound and different words from the Methodist song. The words in this song say,

[Selection 24]

> *Jesus is standing in the water.*
> *Jesus is standing in the water.*
> *He is the Savior and He is standing in the water.*
> *He has given all people a road to follow to heaven.*
> *He gave this road to all people; He is in heaven.*

Both the Methodists and Baptists used to sing these baptism songs quite often. But today, you don't hear these hymns much anymore. Only a few ministers and their church congregations sing them just every once in a while.

The third song I've sung here is another one of Francis Tsonetokoy's songs. It is the song that Eric featured in the second chapter of this book. The words, once again, translate into English as,

[Selection 25]

> *It is good that God made my spirit feel good. I am glad.*
> *It is Him: He is the One who made my spirit feel good. I am glad.*
> *It is good that God made my spirit feel good.*
> *One day, I felt so bad and so lonely.*
> *It is good that God made my spirit feel good.*
>
> *It is Him: He is the One who made my spirit feel good. I am glad.*
> *It is good that God made my spirit feel good.*
> *One day, I felt so bad and so lonely.*
> *It is good that God made my spirit feel good.*

I wanted to include this song because I consider my uncle Francis to be one of the best Kiowa hymn singers that ever lived. It just seemed like songs would come to him. His thoughts were always that way.

When Francis lost his wife, he felt so bad. He didn't want to remarry because his relationship with his wife was forever. When this song first came to him (see the second chapter), he sang it for me. I understood why this song would come to him, but I didn't exactly *feel* what he meant. Now that I've lost my own wife, Mildred, I know exactly what he means in this song. I have a deeper sense of the mixed emotions when one loses their companion. Today, sometimes I too feel so lonely, and so depressed, just like my uncle did. Now, when I sing this hymn, it takes on a whole new meaning. Yes, this song ministers to me. And it uplifts me.

SELECTION 26

Ralph Kotay and his Kiowa hymn class, March 1994

This last song, we sing it just about anywhere for any occasion. It's a beautiful song. It has been sung for many, many years. And everybody just loves this song. So I try to sing it as often as I can. It's called the Kiowa Prayer Song:

> *Let us all pray to God.*
> *Let us all pray to God.*
> *He will open the heavenly doors for you.*
> *And you all will feel good.*
> *He will give you everlasting life.*
> *And you will be forever happy.*

The songs that I've presented here only represent just a few of our Kiowa hymns. We have many of these songs. I've recorded as many as I can for my classes. In fact, after the first year of meeting, we had only gotten through a fraction of them. I made some recordings that were produced by Indian Sounds a few years back. There are seventy-seven songs on those tapes alone. And we didn't even produce all the songs that I sang for *those* tapes.

Many people have learned Kiowa hymns from my recordings. And I'm glad of that. I'm especially glad that my students have been concerned enough to come to my classes and record my singing, because later on in life we're not going to have the song leaders we have today. We have many other Kiowa song leaders like me. I'm not the only one. But most of us, we want the songs to go on. We're trying to get our younger people to understand these things; we don't want this to die out. Not many young people are singing these songs anymore. At some churches, they don't sing the old traditional hymns at all. They sing English hymns and gospel instead. That's good, of course, because those songs are praising the Lord, too. But these Kiowa hymns are special. It's just like I *always* say to my students: If you're really a true believer, you're sincere about Christianity, these songs will somehow work with you. The words are *so* precious. The words get you to start thinking about your own life. That's the way *all* these songs are, no matter what tribe you're from.[6]

Luke Eric Lassiter, Clyde Ellis, and Ralph Kotay

Afterword

On the Study of American Indian Christianity

𝄢 On a cold and snowy evening just a few days after Christmas 2000, Donna Kotay sat talking at her dinner table about her father's love of Kiowa hymns. "I have a lot of respect for my dad and what he's done," she said. "As far back as I can remember, my dad has sung church songs. . . .

"My dad teaches these songs because he doesn't want them dying out. He doesn't want people to lose that, because this is going to be it, as far as he's concerned. He's concerned that we're going to lose our—he calls it—our 'Kiowa identity.' If we lose our songs and we lose our language, there's not going to be anything, except for our name, 'Kiowa.' That's why he's always taught these songs."

Donna continued to talk about the many classes that Ralph has taught over the years. After several minutes, she began to talk about this particular project, *The Jesus Road.* "To me," she said as she placed her hand on an earlier draft of the manuscript, "this is his way of trying to preserve part of our heritage. It's his way of trying to make people know that this is important. . . .

"See, this *matters* because if the songs don't keep going, they'll die out and we won't have any Kiowa hymns. And if our Kiowa hymns go, our language will go also, because our language is intertwined with our Kiowa hymns. Every Kiowa hymn that you hear has a meaning behind it. Once that Kiowa hymn goes, it's probably not going to be brought back."

Theresa Carter, who sat across the table from Donna, echoed Donna's sentiments: "Those songs are straight from the heart. Somebody's experience. Somebody's vision. And it just came to them. . . . It was *because* of that experience and whatever feeling they had from God at that time. They're straight from the heart. . . .

"Those early Christians were true Christians because they were converted to Christianity . . . and they took it into their heart and became Christians," Theresa continued. "These songs are their experiences, their religious experiences. It's what these songs *are*. . . . That's why we listen to these songs and think so much of those early Christians. Like when they say, 'His mother made that song' after a certain experience. It was true to the heart. She experienced something and the song came out. It was her religious experience, and most of these songs are just that. They *are* the miracles."

"These songs were given to them from God," said Donna after a while. "They came from God. Because all of a sudden, their eyes were opened and they saw God. There's a Spirit, and it just moves through them. It's just something that happens to them, and it's got to come out. And it comes out in song."[1]

Christian Experience, Kiowa Song, and Collaborative Ethnography

Beginning in the fall of 2000, when we finished the first draft of the manuscript for this book, we began to solicit comments from people in the Kiowa community about the way we had represented Kiowa Christian experience and Indian hymns in this text. In addition to reworking quotes and adding and subtracting material at our consultants' request, our ultimate goal was to find ways to deepen our interpretations through a broader discussion of the text—a writing approach often called reciprocal or collaborative ethnography.[2]

Our responses were varied, of course, but most of these conversations eventually led to discussions about the importance of maintaining the practice of Kiowa song, as Donna and Theresa express in the conversation above. Significantly, many of our consultants echoed the assertion that much more was at stake than language or song itself. The larger memory and experience of a very particular spiritual encounter—the miracles expressed in song, to paraphrase Theresa—are also at stake.

Many readers may not fully appreciate these sentiments. Yet these convictions should not be underestimated. We all live in a world in which the transformations of critical human institutions such as family, community, and local tradition continue to accommodate a rapidly changing world outside the limits of our control. And indigenous languages are no exception. Unfortunately for us all, with the loss of these languages comes the loss of very particular ways of remembering and expressing a diversity of unfolding human experiences.

Many elderly Kiowa people recognize that they are probably the last generation of fluent speakers of the Kiowa language. Yet they assert, as does Ralph in the preceding pages, that teaching a younger generation to appreciate the language in and surrounding song is key to maintaining a memory of Kiowa Christianity in particular and a larger Kiowa heritage in general. Vincent Bointy, who also teaches a Kiowa hymn and language class, says that "it's important to teach our kids these songs because it gives us the opportunity to talk about our history, our past."[3] For Kiowa Christians, telling this past is critical for communicating the devout and dedicated faith upon which their religious tradition rests. "When I was reading this book," Vincent goes on to say, "when you were talking about the role of Christianity in here, I can't help but think about those old people. They were the true Christians. My parents and grandparents—like Ralph's parents and grandparents—they went through some unbearable hardships to be Christians. Today, *none* of us measure up to what they once were."[4]

Thus, as stated in the introduction, our ultimate purpose for this book has been to help preserve the knowledge surrounding Kiowa hymns. This knowledge, however, is only part of a larger experience. Indeed, many hymns remain unsung and many more stories remain untold. With this in mind, we realize that this work is necessarily incomplete. On a larger community level, the discussion of Kiowa Christian heritage is complex and complicated. There are many singers, churches, congregations, and songs. Songs and stories thus overlap, compete, and differ. Milton Noel, for example, reports that in his church—Rainy Mountain Baptist—many elders still talk about the very first Kiowa hymns. One story stands out. "The missionaries Lauretta E. Ballew and Henrietta Reeside encouraged Gotebo to 'make' a song, to put Kiowa words into a hymn," says Milton, who is Gotebo's great-great-grandson. "But Gotebo refused at first, saying that it would be too much like the old ways. It would sound too much like the old songs. Those ladies kept on him though, and he finally came out with a song; after that, these hymns just took off. That 'first hymn,' as we call it at Rainy Mountain— it's selection 20 in your book." [5]

Stories like this are many and diverse. People disagree, for example, about when and where Kiowas first sang their own Christian hymns. Regardless of such differences, however, a diversity of interpretations and tellings attests to the fact that many people remain committed to maintaining both song and heritage from a number of different perspectives. While songs and stories may overlap, compete, or differ, in the end Indian hymns remain in the Kiowa community as powerful testimonies for articulating what it means to be Kiowa today. "There's a feeling you get from a Kiowa hymn," says Frances Doyebi, after reading a draft of the manuscript for this book. "There are some that hit you just right. The words in that song are what you are feeling, you know. They have a really special meaning. Sometimes you feel like crying or sometimes it's just a glad feeling. And you always know that there's a song for that special occasion. And this is what Ralph is trying to get across here. . . .

"These songs stay with you," Frances continued. "When my mother was sick, I sang a song all the time, a song that says 'God be with us. Bring us through this.' And even now when they sing it in church, I can feel that. I tried so hard for my mother, with this song that I sang over and over. It's songs like that that stay with you. At certain times, somebody might come in and sing a song for you when you're sick or something, and that song will hit you. And knowing God, and being a Christian, it really means something to you. It may not mean anything to anyone else. But it means something to you, as a Kiowa person."[6]

Thanks to elderly singers and their efforts to teach songs to a new generation, these songs are living on for the time being. As Anita Black-bear says, "I think a lot of younger people are starting to show more interest in these hymns. They're thankful that they have a heritage and a culture, and that they know who they are. It's very important to know where they come from. That's the beauty of it right there."[7]

On the Implications of Studying American Indian Christianity

Some of the most profound changes experienced in Native North America over the last several centuries have been religious; indeed, Christianity has had an enormous impact on Indian communities.[8] Yet the scholarly descriptions and understandings of these changes have been largely (but certainly not entirely) dictated by academically positioned models, models like "assimilation" that emphasize broad, sweeping changes and ignore the deeper experiential complexities that have emerged from this multidimensional encounter.[9]

This multidimensional encounter is an important matter, for the history of missions in Indian country has too often been disparaged as little more than an exercise in genocide or a horror from which Indians have hardly recovered. Robin Fisher, for example, has written that "the demands of missionaries could not be incorporated into existing Indian society; their teaching and example had to be either accepted or rejected, and acceptance meant virtually a total culture change for the proselyte."[10] While it is certainly true that some missionaries had an antagonistic relationship with Indians (Marcus and Narcissa Whitman, Presbyterian missionaries among the Cayuse, come to mind), it is also true that in case after case, missionaries and Indians forged deeply meaningful relationships that did not require Indians to surrender their identity or even their beliefs. "One might assume," writes Jack Schultz, "that 'Christian' is synonymous with assimilated, that is, that by adopting this foreign faith, the natives have lost their native soul . . . if not their whole identity." But because such thinking relies on assimilation, acculturation, and ethnicity models based on "traditional" traits, it is easy—and misleading—to trot out lists of what has been lost in the wake of the missions. But to do this is to miss the point entirely, for what ultimately matters in these encounters is how Indians and missionaries alike responded to a "shared history of interaction, communication, negotiation, and face-to-face encounters . . . not a fixed set of traits, behaviors, structures, or modes of production."[11] To speak only of cultural loss is to ignore the fact that culture is a human construction that changes as a matter of purpose. Too often, discussions of the missions suggest that such change was largely if not entirely corrosive, coercive, and unilateral.

On closer inspection, what often emerges in the stories of missions in Indian country is a complicated narrative dominated by negotiations and accommodations on all sides. It would be folly to suggest that each group gave in gracefully and met in the middle on every difficult issue, but there is too much evidence of Christianity's importance and deep meaning in the Indian community to disregard the degree to which tribes made room for this new faith in order to gain or maintain some sense of control. Thus, listening to Native peoples speak of this history is crucial to our understanding of how and why they accepted religious practices that were new and, frankly, sometimes at odds with their traditional ways. Importantly, it also makes them the central players in that history, actors with agency who understood what they were doing. James Treat acknowledges that it is easy to think of Native Christianity as "historically and culturally problematic," but he adds that its very existence forces scholars to reckon with how and why it became so important to Indians. The answer, in part, is that Native Christians

constructed and maintained their . . . religious identities with a variety of considerations in mind. Like native traditions, Christian traditions can mediate social power and material resources and provide avenues for the development and recognition of religious leadership. Like native traditions, Christian liturgical forms can facilitate community reconciliation and allow for the fulfillment of ceremonial obligations. Like native traditions, Christian teachings can articulate beliefs and values that provide direction in daily life and in overcoming personal struggles. . . . Furthermore, many native Christians accomplish this identification without abandoning or rejecting native religious traditions. . . . To dismiss all native Christians as acculturated . . . is to miss innumerable demonstrations of their insightful historical and social analysis, their complex and sophisticated religious creativity, and their powerful devotion to personal and community survival.[12]

Thus, understanding the deeper significance of Indian hymns—in this case, Kiowa hymns—opens a window onto the multifaceted intersection between Christianity and American Indian experience. When one listens to Kiowa people talk about Indian hymns coupled with the voices from past and present described in part 1, models like assimilation do more to obscure encounter and experience than to elaborate on it. When scholars begin to consider more deeply the intersection of Christianity and American Indian identity through the lens of experience, a more elaborate understanding of Native American Christian identity in general and Kiowa Christian identity in particular begins to unfold. In the end, when Native American studies scholars consider the history of missions in Indian country, they must reconceptualize and describe experience and identity in more complex ways. As James Clifford writes, "Stories of cultural contact and change have been structured by a pervasive dichotomy: absorption by the other *or* resistance to the other. . . . Yet what if identity is conceived not as a boundary to be maintained but as a nexus of relations and transactions actively engaging a subject? The story or stories of interaction must then be more complex, less linear and teleological."[13] Expounding upon the language in and surrounding Indian hymns, we believe, invokes stories of interaction that are necessarily more complex and less linear and teleological than that often portrayed in the literature. Indeed, historians, anthropologists, ethnomusicologists, and folklorists have written little about Indian hymns compared to what they have written about so-called "traditional songs." It often seems that Christian song repertoires are regarded as less traditional, less Indian, and therefore less "Other." The result? As Thomas McElwain argues in writing about Iroquois Christian hymns, "Researchers have been blind to a rich source of information on native spirituality in the native Christian traditions."[14]

How do scholars correct this blind spot? How might we enhance our understanding of Indian hymns, experience, and Native American Christian identity—not just in the Kiowa community or the southern plains, but in all Native communities? On a broad level, we should continue the work of examining the epistemological assumptions concerning culture, change, and identity. More to the point, however, the struggle of ethnographic understanding—that of being fully committed to elaborating the "native point of view" within a collaborative ethnographic framework—continues to offer the most viable model for positively complicating and enriching the wider conversation about Native American experience and identity. Conceptualized in this way, the engagement of American Indian Christianity has the potential to further broaden the framework of our discussions about culture to aggressively include ethnographic consultants—who in their talk about God, encounter, and experience force us to reconsider how academics have traditionally understood Native American Christian identity. When, for example, Vincent Bointy suggests that "we lost our Christianity because we turned towards the white man's ways" (see part 1), one is immediately forced to reexamine the limitations of academically constructed models originally founded on assimilation and consider instead the nexus of relations and transactions that engender the meanings of American Indian Christian heritage expressed in language and song.[15]

Notes

INTRODUCTION

1. For a more in-depth discussion of these events, see Ellis, "'She Gave Us the Jesus Way,'" v–xxii.

2. Margaret O'Pry, Dean Reeder, and Bell Reeder, recorded conversation with Luke Eric Lassiter and Clyde Ellis, Saddle Mountain, Oklahoma, 11 June 1998.

3. Herbert Westner, recorded conversation with Luke Eric Lassiter, Ralph Kotay, and Clyde Ellis, Cache, Oklahoma, 10 June 1998.

4. Ralph and I, for example, discussed the book for a review. See Luke E. Lassiter, review of *Kiowa: A Woman Missionary* in *American Indian Quarterly* 22, no. 4 (1998): 498–99.

5. See Lassiter, *The Power of Kiowa Song*, 139–52.

6. See the afterword for further discussion on this matter. Compare Schröder, "From Parkman to Postcolonial Theory." See also Schultz, *The Seminole Baptist Churches*, 5–9.

7. In addition, Crawford's story has already been told. See Ellis, "'She Gave Us the Jesus Way.'"

8. See, e.g., Kotay, *Kiowa Hymns Sung by Ralph Kotay* (cassette).

9. The Kiowa history that I have presented here is admittedly very brief and incomplete; for a fuller description, see Mooney, *Calendar History*. Additionally, Kiowa history is closely tied to Comanche and Kiowa-Apache histories, a historical and cultural relationship to which I only allude. For other treatments of Kiowa, Comanche, and Apache histories, see Battey, *The Life and Adventures of a Quaker among the Indians;* Boyd, *Kiowa*

Voices; Ellis, *To Change Them Forever;* Ewers, *Murals in the Round;* Foster, *Being Comanche;* Hagan, *United States–Comanche Relations;* Kavanagh, *Comanche Political History;* Kracht, "Kiowa Religion: An Ethnohistorical Analysis"; Levy, "After Custer"; Marriott, *The Ten Grandmothers;* Mayhall, *The Kiowas;* McBeth, *Ethnic Identity and the Boarding School Experience of West-Central Oklahoma American Indians;* Meadows, *Kiowa, Apache, and Comanche Military Societies;* Mishkin, *Rank and Warfare;* Momaday, *The Way to Rainy Mountain;* Noyes, *Los Comanches;* Nye, *Carbine and Lance;* Parsons, *Kiowa Tales;* Jane Richardson, *Law and Status among the Kiowa Indians;* Tatum, *Our Red Brothers;* Paul Anthony Vestal and Richard Evans Schultes, *The Economic Botany of the Kiowa Indians: As It Relates to the History of the Tribe* (New York: AMS Press, 1981); and Wallace and Hoebel, *The Comanches.*

10. Mooney, *Calendar History,* 159–62.
11. Wallace and Hoebel, *The Comanches,* 1–12.
12. Mooney, *Calendar History,* 162–65.
13. Mooney, *Calendar History,* 162–65; see also Wallace and Hoebel, *The Comanches,* 12.
14. See Mishkin, *Rank and Warfare.*
15. See Ellis, *To Change Them Forever,* 28–53; Hagan, *United States–Comanche Relations,* 1–2.
16. See Hagan, *United States–Comanche Relations,* 1–26.
17. See Hagan, *United States–Comanche Relations,* 27–43; Mooney, *Calendar History,* 178–80.
18. Hagan, *United States–Comanche Relations,* 42; Mooney, *Calendar History,* 181–219.
19. See Mooney, *Calendar History,* 221–23. See also Kracht, "Kiowa Religion: An Ethnohistorical Analysis"; Kracht, "The Kiowa Ghost Dance"; Lassiter, *The Power of Kiowa Song;* Moses, *The Indian Man,* 179–206; and Omer C. Stewart, *Peyote Religion: A History* (Norman: University of Oklahoma Press, 1987).
20. See Ellis, *To Change Them Forever;* Hagan, *United States–Comanche Relations,* 120–200; and Prucha, *The Great Father,* 1:501–33.
21. See Clark, *Lone Wolf v. Hitchcock;* Hagan, *United States–Comanche Rela-*

tions, 201–61; Mooney, *Calendar History*, 224–25; and Prucha, *The Great Father*, 2:659–86.

22. The discussion that follows relies heavily on Prucha, *The Great Father*, and especially Prucha, *The Indians in American Society*, 28ff.

23. Prucha, *The Indians in American Society*, 55–79. See also Muriel H. Wright, *A Guide to the Indian Tribes of Oklahoma* (1951; reprint, Norman: University of Oklahoma Press, 1986), 127, 176, 178.

24. Prucha, *The Indians in American Society*, 68–103. See also Horse and Lassiter, "A Tribal Chair's Perspective on Inherent Sovereignty."

25. See Lassiter, *The Power of Kiowa Song*, 69ff.

THE JESUS ROAD

1. Recorded conversations with Luke Eric Lassiter and Clyde Ellis: Vincent Bointy and Cornelius Spottedhorse, Carnegie, Oklahoma, 12 June 1998; Cy Hall Zotigh, Saddle Mountain, Oklahoma, 11 June 1998.

2. Omboke quoted in Hayne, *Kiowa Turning*, 26.

3. Stumbling Bear quoted in Forbes, "John Jasper Methvin," 73.

4. Prucha, *The Great Father*, 1:146; Berkhofer, *Salvation and the Savage*, 10.

5. Bowden, *American Indians and Christian Missions*, 164–65; missionary quote in Berkhofer, *Salvation and the Savage*, 10.

6. Taylor quote in Prucha, *The Great Father*, 1:488; *Annual Report of the Board of Indian Commissioners*, 1869, quoted in Prucha, *The Great Father*, 1:510.

7. Doolittle Committee report quote in Keller, *American Protestantism*, 9–10 (emphasis in the original); Indian Peace Commission report quote in Prucha, ed., *Documents of United States Indian Policy*, 106.

8. Doolittle Committee quote, 104, and Indian Peace Commission quote, 108–9, both in Prucha, ed., *Documents of United States Indian Policy*; Prucha, *The Great Father*, 1:491.

9. Prucha, *The Great Father*, 1:512–13; Tatum, *Our Red Brothers*, 17–18.

10. U. S. Grant, "First Inaugural Address," in James D. Richardson, ed., *A Compilation of the Messages and Papers of the Presidents* (New York: Bureau of National Literature, 1897), 8:3962 (hereafter cited as *Messages and Papers of the Presidents*); Quakers quoted in Keller, *American Protestantism*, 12, 16; Prucha, *The Great Father*, 1:502–3.

11. U. S. Grant, "First Annual Message," *Messages and Papers of the Presidents*, 9:3992–93; Prucha, *The Great Father*, 1:503. For discussions of the Peace Policy, see Keller, *American Protestantism*, 16–30; Milner, *With Good Intentions*, 1–26; Prucha, *American Indian Policy in Crisis*, 33–71.

12. United States, Office of Indian Affairs, *Annual Report of the Commissioner of Indian Affairs to the Secretary of the Interior* (Washington DC: Government Printing Office), 1870, 474; 1872, 461–62 (hereafter cited as *ARCIA* with year).

13. Delano quoted in Hagan, *United States–Comanche Relations*, 77; *ARCIA*, 1871, 3–4.

14. Keller, *American Protestantism*, 134.

15. Mooney, *Calendar History*, 226; Tatum, *Our Red Brothers*, 24, 25, 35; Hagan, "The Reservation Policy," 160. For the history of the Quaker administration of the KCA Reservation, see Keller, *American Protestantism*, 130–48; Cutler, "Lawrie Tatum and the Kiowa Agency"; Steele, "The Beginning of Quaker Administration of Indian Affairs in Oklahoma"; Steele, "Lawrie Tatum's Indian Policy"; Zwink, "On the White Man's Road."

16. Tatum, *Our Red Brothers*, 10, 35; Ellis, *To Change Them Forever*, 31; Hagan, *United States–Comanche Relations*, 61–63; Keller, *American Protestantism*, 134.

17. Keller, *American Protestantism*, 133–35; Tatum, *Our Red Brothers*, xiii, 30.

18. Battey, *The Life and Adventures of a Quaker among the Indians*, 115–35; Ruby W. Shannon, "Friends for the Indians: 100 Years of Education at the Riverside Indian School" (bound ms., n.d., Linschied Library, East Central University, Ada, Oklahoma), 3; Haworth quoted in *ARCIA*, 1873, 588; Josiah Butler, "Pioneer School Teaching at the Comanche-Kiowa Agency School, 1870–1873," *Chronicles of Oklahoma* 8 (1928): 482–528.

19. First Tatum quote in Keller, *American Protestantism*, 134–38; second quote in Ellis, *To Change Them Forever*, 35.

20. "Phil-anthropy" quote in Robert Athearn, *William Tecumseh Sherman and the Settlement of the West* (Norman: University of Oklahoma Press, 1956), 289; "soft-soaping Quakers" and "Quaker hats" quotes in Keller, *American Protestantism*, 137; Kracht, "Kiowa Religion: An Ethnohistorical Analysis," 634; Vernon, "Methodist Beginnings," 395. For a discussion of the collapse of the Peace Policy, see Keller, *American Protestantism*, 90–105, 188–204.

21. Adams, "Fundamental Considerations," 18. On allotment at the KCA Reservation, see Rand, "Negotiating the 'New Country' "; Hagan, *United States–Comanche Relations,* 201–85; Hagan, "Adjusting to the Opening of the Kiowa, Comanche, and Kiowa-Apache Reservation."

22. Methvin, "Reminiscences of Life among the Indians," 178.

23. *Annual Report of the Kiowa Agency,* in ARCIA, 1888, 97.

24. Corwin, "Protestant Missionary Work," 54; Sam L. Botkin, "Indian Missions of the Episcopal Church in Oklahoma," *Chronicles of Oklahoma* 36 (1958): 42; Vernon, "Methodist Beginnings," 402; Herring, "Failed Assimilation," 85–86; Kracht, "Kiowa Religion: An Ethnohistorical Analysis," 638, 1035.

25. The history of Catholic missions at the KCA Reservation has not attracted much attention from scholars. The best account is Kracht, "Kiowa Religion: An Ethnohistorical Analysis," 674–92, on which I have relied heavily. See also Lehman, "Father Isidore Ricklin."

26. Kracht, "Kiowa Religion: An Ethnohistorical Analysis," 675–76; Lehman, "Father Isidore Ricklin," 35–36.

27. Kracht, "Kiowa Religion: An Ethnohistorical Analysis," 677; Lehman, "Father Isidore Ricklin," 36. For a comparison to the often dreadful conditions that prevailed at government schools, see Ellis, " 'A Remedy for Barbarism.' "

28. Kracht, "Kiowa Religion: An Ethnohistorical Analysis," 675–76.

29. Daisey and Jack Hokeah interview, 1 January 1968, T-178, Doris Duke Oral History Collection, Western History Collections, University of Oklahoma, Norman, 2 (hereafter cited as DDOH).

30. Kracht, "Kiowa Religion: An Ethnohistorical Analysis," 677, 682–84.

31. Mausape quoted in Forbes, "John Jasper Methvin," 65. The most complete discussion of Methvin's experiences on the KCA Reservation is Forbes, "John Jasper Methvin," on which I have heavily relied. See also Babcock, "John Jasper Methvin"; Babcock and Bryce, *History of Methodism in Oklahoma,* 231–40; Methvin, *In the Limelight;* Methvin, "Reminiscences of Life among the Indians"; Kracht, "Kiowa Religion: An Ethnohistorical Analysis," 639–53.

32. First five quoted phrases in Methvin, "Reminiscences of Life among the

Indians," 169–70; last quote in Babcock, "John Jasper Methvin," 115–16; Corwin, "Protestant Missionary Work," 43–46.

33. Methvin quote in Forbes, "John Jasper Methvin," 51–52; Vernon, "Methodist Beginnings," 401; Corwin, "Protestant Missionary Work," 46; Methvin, *In the Limelight,* 88–89; Kracht, "Kiowa Religion: An Ethnohistorical Analysis," 646–47.

34. Adams, "Fundamental Considerations," 4–5; Forbes, "John Jasper Methvin," 62–64; Morgan quoted in "Lake Mohonk Conference Proceedings," ARCIA, 1889, 94–95.

35. Methvin quoted in Forbes, "John Jasper Methvin," 52; Vernon, "Methodist Beginnings," 404–5. See also Herring, "Their Work Was Never Done."

36. Methvin, "Reminiscences of Life among the Indians," 177–78; Forbes, "John Jasper Methvin," 71–72.

37. Bointy and Spottedhorse recorded conversation; Nye, *Carbine and Lance,* 267.

38. Methvin, "Reminiscences of Life among the Indians," 174; Methvin, *Andele, or, The Mexican-Kiowa Captive;* Vernon, "Methodist Beginnings," 397–99, 401–9; Kracht, "Kiowa Religion: An Ethnohistorical Analysis," 639–40.

39. Kracht, "Kiowa Religion: An Ethnohistorical Analysis," 650–53.

40. All quotes in Methvin, *In the Limelight,* 89–91; Forbes, "John Jasper Methvin," 65; Leland Clegg and William B. Odom, *Oklahoma Methodism in the Twentieth Century* (Nashville TN: Parthenon Press, 1968), 91; Kracht, "Kiowa Religion: An Ethnohistorical Analysis," 682–83.

41. Stecker quote in Kracht, "Kiowa Religion: An Ethnohistorical Analysis," 685, 688; *Interpreter* (February/March 1998) at *www.interpretermagazine.org/febmar98/cover3.htm,* 2.

42. Stecker and Gassoway quotes in Kracht, "Kiowa Religion: An Ethnohistorical Analysis," 686, 687; Methvin quote in Methvin, *In the Limelight,* 88.

43. Kracht, "Kiowa Religion: An Ethnohistorical Analysis," 685–86.

44. Kracht, "Kiowa Religion: An Ethnohistorical Analysis," 913–17.

45. *Interpreter* (February/March 1998); Oklahoma Indian Mission Conference homepage at *www.umc.org;* M. Stewart, "The Indian Mission Conference of Oklahoma," 334.

46. E. C. Routh, *The Story of Oklahoma Baptists* (Oklahoma City: Baptist Gen-

eral Convention, 1932), 60. For the history of Baptist missions at the KCA Reservation, see Corwin, "Protestant Missionary Work"; Kracht, "Kiowa Religion: An Ethnohistorical Analysis," 660–74; Hayne, *Kiowa Turning;* Dane, "History of Baptist Missions"; Robert Hamilton, *The Gospel among the Red Man* (Knoxville TN: Sunday School Board of the Southern Baptist Convention, 1930), 203–11; Ellis, " 'She Gave Us the Jesus Way,' " v–xxii.

47. All quotations from Dane, "History of Baptist Missions," 29, 38.

48. Ellis, *To Change Them Forever*, 43, 75; Crawford, *Joyful Journey*, 54–55.

49. Lone Wolf quote in Hayne, *Kiowa Turning*, 14–15, 17; ReQua quote in Dane, "History of Baptist Missions," 43; Corwin, "Protestant Missionary Work," 49.

50. Hayne, *Kiowa Turning*, 17.

51. Anonymous quotes in Burdette, *Young Women among Blanket Indians*, 6, 20; Hicks and Murrow quotes in Dane, "History of Baptist Missions," 42, 45–46; Kiowas' quotes in Hayne, *Kiowa Turning*, 25; Quanah Parker quote in "The Kiowa Indians, Early Beginnings of Baptist Missionary Work," n.d., Indian Missions Correspondence Files for Oklahoma, American Baptist Archives, Valley Forge PA, 19.

52. Lone Wolf quote in Hayne, *Kiowa Turning*, 25; "joy and gratitude" quote in Dane, "History of Baptist Missions," 46; Big Tree quote in Burdette, *Young Women among Blanket Indians*, 12, 18.

53. Burdette, *Young Women among Blanket Indians*, 33–36, 45 (Reeside quote); Hayne, *Kiowa Turning*, 18, 20.

54. Ernestine Kauahquo Kauley interview, 8 April 1967, T-43, DDOH, 12–13.

55. Burdette, *Young Women among Blanket Indians*, 49; Dane, "History of Baptist Missions," 47–48.

56. Dane, "History of Baptist Missions," 48; Hamilton, *The Gospel among the Red Man*, 205–7.

57. Ellis, " 'She Gave Us the Jesus Way,' " viii–xii. Crawford recounted her experiences in two books, *Joyful Journey* and *Kiowa: The History of a Blanket Indian Mission* (New York: Fleming H. Revell, 1915), which was compiled from her private journals. (The latter was reprinted in 1998 as *Kiowa: A Woman Missionary in Indian Territory.*) See also Corwin, "Saddle Mountain Mission and Church"; Morrison, "Isabel Crawford: Missionary to the Kiowa Indians."

58. Anonymous quote in *The Heroine of Saddle Mountain,* 18; Mary Aitson, telephone conversation with Clyde Ellis, 20 July 1998. (The family changed the spelling of its name from Aitsan to Aitson in the twentieth century.)

59. Kracht, "Kiowa Religion: An Ethnohistorical Analysis," 927; Kroeker, *Comanches and Mennonites on the Oklahoma Plains,* 20.

60. First Crawford quote in Ellis, " 'She Gave Us the Jesus Way,' " xv (emphasis in the original); second quote in *The Heroine of Saddle Mountain,* 28.

61. Ellis, " 'She Gave Us the Jesus Way,' " v.

62. Dane, "History of Baptist Missions," 114–15, 205–8.

63. Oklahoma Indian Baptist Association statements quoted in Dane, "History of Baptist Missions," 73, 104; Omboke quoted in Hayne, *Kiowa Turning,* 26.

64. Mooney, *Calendar History,* 220, 349–50.

65. Moses, *The Indian Man,* 59–60; Mooney, *Calendar History,* 359–60; Crawford, *Kiowa,* 27–28.

66. Moses, *The Indian Man,* 179–211.

67. Forbes, "John Jasper Methvin," 70.

68. Crawford, *Kiowa,* 139, 184–85.

69. DeMallie, ed., *The Sixth Grandfather,* 15.

70. Kenneth M. Morrison, "Montagnais Missionization in Early New France: The Syncretic Imperative," *American Indian Culture and Research Journal* 10 (1986): 1; James P. Ronda, "Generations of Faith: The Christian Indians of Martha's Vineyard," *William and Mary Quarterly* 38 (1980): 369–94; Kidwell, *Choctaws and Missionaries in Mississippi,* 180, 183. See also Sergei Kan's *Memory Eternal,* in which he notes that conversion "rarely involves a total change of heart but [is] a subtle process of negotiation and compromise, acceptance of some aspects of the new ideology and rejection of others" (xx).

71. Ioleta Hunt McElhaney interview, 3 March 1968, T-198-1, DDOH, 6.

72. Odlepaugh quoted in Crawford, *Kiowa,* 235; Black Elk quoted in DeMallie, ed., *The Sixth Grandfather,* 17.

73. Cecil Horse interview, 13 June 1967, T-27, DDOH, 20–22.

74. Vernon, "Methodist Beginnings," 398; Corwin, "Protestant Missionary Work," 47; anonymous quote in Babcock, "John Jasper Methvin," 116–17; Methvin, "Reminiscences of Life among the Indians," 172.

75. Crawford, *Kiowa*, 140; Kauley interview, 14.

76. Anonymous quote in Forbes, "John Jasper Methvin," 68, 72; Kracht, "Kiowa Religion: An Ethnohistorical Analysis," 642.

77. Methvin and Mausape quoted in Forbes, "John Jasper Methvin," 63, 65; *The Heroine of Saddle Mountain*, 28; the Beckers quoted in Kroeker, *Comanches and Mennonites*, 141.

78. Sherman Chaddlesone, "The Old Indians Called Her 'Woman with a Brave Heart,' " 1942, Indian Missions Correspondence Files for Oklahoma, American Baptist Archives, Valley Forge PA, 4–7.

79. Bointy and Spottedhorse recorded conversation.

80. Crawford, *Kiowa*, 187.

81. Crawford, *Kiowa*, 17; Setainte's widow quoted in Hayne, *Kiowa Turning*, 22.

82. Crawford, *Kiowa*, 25; Comanche man quoted in Burdette, *Young Women among Blanket Indians*, 60; Asenap quoted in Kroeker, *Comanches and Mennonites*, 28, see also 96–97.

83. Onko and anonymous man quoted in Ellis, " 'She Gave Us the Jesus Way,' " xix–xx n.1; Aitson telephone conversation.

84. O'Pry, Reeder, and Reeder recorded conversation.

85. Ioleta Hunt McElhaney interview, 7 July 1969, T-474-1, DDOH, 3; McElhaney interview, T-198-1, 7–8.

86. Helene Fletcher, telephone conversation with Clyde Ellis, 20 July 1998; Daisey and Jack Hokeah interview, 1; Kroeker, *Comanches and Mennonites*, 123.

87. Ralph Kotay, recorded conversation with Luke Eric Lassiter, Apache, Oklahoma, 11 June 1998; Bointy and Spottedhorse recorded conversation; Kroeker, *Comanches and Mennonites*, 138.

88. Bointy and Spottedhorse recorded conversation; Harry Tofpi, conversation with Clyde Ellis, 11 April 1994; Fletcher telephone conversation.

89. O'Pry, Reeder, and Reeder recorded conversation; Zotigh recorded conversation; Dane, "History of Baptist Missions," 163–66.

90. Kracht, "Kiowa Religion: An Ethnohistorical Analysis," 920–21.

91. Kracht, "Kiowa Religion: An Ethnohistorical Analysis," 921.

92. Foster, *Being Comanche*, 126–27.

93. Kracht, "Kiowa Religion in Historical Perspective," 28; Zotigh recorded conversation.

94. Anonymous quote in Kracht, "Kiowa Religion: An Ethnohistorical Analysis," 919–20; Zotigh recorded conversation; Bointy and Spottedhorse recorded conversation; McElhaney interview, T-198-1, 6–7.
95. Kracht, "Kiowa Religion in Historical Perspective," 27.
96. Zotigh recorded conversation; Bointy and Spottedhorse recorded conversation.

INDIAN CHURCHES AND INDIAN HYMNS

1. This song is also featured on the accompanying compact disc, selection 1.
2. Recorded conversation, Ralph Kotay's Kiowa hymn class, Anadarko, Oklahoma, 4 January 1994.
3. It should go without saying that Native American people in southwestern Oklahoma also attend non-Indian and other community churches. I should note here that many Catholics attend masses in southwestern Oklahoma that generally include people from a variety of backgrounds, not just Native American. "Indian churches," as the term is used in southwestern Oklahoma, most often denotes Protestant denominations, and the term "Indian hymns" denotes those songs sung in these congregations. Drawing from my experience and research in southwestern Oklahoma—particularly concerning Kiowa hymns—the rest of my discussion will follow along these lines. For a more in-depth discussion of the historical context surrounding Kiowa churches and hymns in southwestern Oklahoma, see, for example, Boyd, *Kiowa Voices;* Ellis, " 'She Gave Us the Jesus Way,' " v–xxii; and Kracht, "Kiowa Religion: An Ethnohistorical Analysis."
4. While these modes of musical expression are the norm in most church services, in some instructional contexts (such as Ralph's class), singers may sing from written sources. Among Kiowas, for example, the pamphlet entitled *Kawy-dawkhyah: Kiowa Christian Songs,* compiled by the Summer Institute of Linguistics in Norman, Oklahoma, and published by Wycliffe Bible Translators—usually in photocopied form—features seventy songs written phonetically in the Kiowa language with translations in English. The publication circulates among many song leaders and congregations throughout the Kiowa community. But because neither notation nor a recording accompanies the booklet, one must turn to song leaders like Ralph to hear how the featured songs should sound.

5. Hymns sung in southwestern Oklahoma have a variety of forms (e.g., AABCD, ABCD, ABCB, ABCDC BCDC, AABBCD BBCD, and AABCD CD). In their performance, however, they are generally sung in one of two ways. In the first form, a singer sings all the stanzas through to complete the first rendition of the song, then repeats all the stanzas again, over and over, until the song's conclusion (i.e., it is a "complete repetition"). An example is transcribed in this chapter's opening vignette. Each time the stanzas are completed in their entirety, the song is considered sung through once.

In the second form of performance, the singer repeats one or more of the previously sung stanzas (i.e., it is an "incomplete repetition"). An example is transcribed in the next section, "The Words Are *So* Precious: On Language and Story." Unlike the first form of performance, when both sets of stanzas are completed, here the song is considered sung through twice. Structurally, these latter forms are much like other American Indian songs from the Great Plains tribes (e.g., War Dance songs).

6. Kotay recorded conversation, 11 June 1998.

7. Relatively little has been written on Indian hymns, but see, for example, Giglio, *Southern Cheyenne Women's Songs,* 163–206; Lassiter, *The Power of Kiowa Song,* 139–52; McElwain, " 'The Rainbow Will Carry Me' "; and Smyth, *Songs of Indian Territory,* 64–67.

8. Ralph Kotay, recorded conversation with Luke Eric Lassiter, Apache, Oklahoma, 6 September 1994. Hymn repertoires in southwestern Oklahoma are distinguished from one another by their language texts and are thus assigned to the different tribal song repertoires of which they are a part. Further distinctions within a particular hymn repertoire do indeed exist—such as that between Kiowa Methodist and Baptist hymns—but these distinctions come with identification only. That is, they are not inherently or structurally Methodist or Baptist but only identified as such.

9. This song is featured on the accompanying compact disc, selection 25.

10. Recorded conversation, Ralph Kotay's Kiowa hymn class, Anadarko, Oklahoma, 28 December 1993. I have chosen not to block long quotations from my consultants as subtext. Instead, I have placed them here within the context of dialogue with the main text.

11. Excerpted from Lassiter, *The Power of Kiowa Song*, 133. The speaker is anonymous.

12. Recorded conversation, Ralph Kotay's Kiowa hymn class, Anadarko, Oklahoma, 25 January 1994. Generally, three types of Kiowa hymns have come through the Spirit. First, the vast majority of Kiowa hymns have Kiowa language texts and are monophonic with a generally descending melodic contour (although there are exceptions to this rule). These songs are sung in church services most often and are sung without accompaniment (except, as stated earlier, in some Pentecostal congregations where members may use a small hand drum to keep time with the song). Second, a very few songs have English tunes (such as "Amazing Grace") with original Kiowa texts—that is, texts that are not translations of the original English text but new textual compositions. These songs are sung only occasionally in church services today and may be sung with or without accompaniment (e.g., a piano). As in other American Indian communities, these songs were most probably the first Christian hymns to be introduced (see Smyth, *Songs of Indian Territory*, 65). But as Ralph says, "the missionaries . . . brought us their songs with the English tunes, but they really didn't catch on. We had our own way of singing" (see selections 4–6 in the chapter "Kiowa Hymns and Their Deeper Meanings" in this book). Third and finally, in some congregations Kiowa hymns and their original texts have been adapted to other song traditions, for example, set to Western notation (see, e.g., "Daw-Kee, Aim Daw-Tsi-Taw [Great Spirit, Now I Pray]," hymn 330 in *The United Methodist Hymnal*), modified for church choir performance, or interpreted through the gospel tradition. These songs are few and seem rarely to be performed in church services.

13. See Lassiter, *The Power of Kiowa Song*, 200ff.

14. Kotay recorded conversation, 6 September 1994.

15. See Lassiter, *The Power of Kiowa Song*, 187ff.

16. Recorded conversation, Ralph Kotay's Kiowa hymn class, 25 January 1994.

17. Kotay recorded conversation, 6 September 1994.

18. Recorded conversation with Anita Blackbear, Ralph Kotay's Kiowa hymn class, 25 January 1994, as excerpted from Lassiter, *The Power of Kiowa Song*, 139.

19. Recorded conversation, Ralph Kotay's Kiowa hymn class, 25 January 1994.

KIOWA HYMNS AND THEIR DEEPER MEANINGS

The compact disc is a compilation of field recordings, and, consequently, the selections vary in their quality and length. Ralph Kotay and I compiled and edited the following first-person discussion primarily from our recorded conversations and telephone conversations, interviews with Ralph conducted by the Oklahoma Folk Arts Council and the Oklahoma Historical Society, and recorded class presentations. All the original sources are as follows:

– Recorded conversations with Ralph Kotay (recorded by Luke Eric Lassiter): 15 July 1992; 14 July 1994; 18 July 1994; 6 September 1994; 22 June 1997; 28 July 1997; 11 June 1998 (with Clyde Ellis); 13 June 1998; 20 June 1998; 2 April 1999; 21 June 2000; 23 June 2000.

– Telephone conversations with Ralph Kotay: 6 June 2000 and 11 July 2000.

– Class presentations by Ralph Kotay (recorded by Luke Eric Lassiter unless otherwise noted): 25 May 1993; 1 June 1993; 3 June 1993; 15 June 1993; 22 June 1993; 29 June 1993; 6 July 1993; 13 July 1993; 20 July 1993; 28 December 1993; 4 January 1994; 25 January 1994; 1 February 1994; 15 February 1994; 22 February 1994; 22 March 1994; 6 April 1994; 19 April 1994; 26 April 1994; 3 May 1994; 17 May 1994; 18 October 1994 (recorded by Danieala Vickers); and 25 October 1994 (recorded by Danieala Vickers).

– Interview with Ralph Kotay by the Oklahoma Historical Society (recorded by Rodger Harris): 27 May 1997 (Tribal Songs Project 97.029, Oklahoma Historical Society, Oklahoma City).

– Interview with Ralph Kotay by the Oklahoma Folk Arts Council (interviewer unknown [as of this writing, these recordings are archived at the Oklahoma Historical Society but uncataloged]): 7 September 1988 and 9 July 1993.

Using these recordings we assembled a text that we felt best articulated Ralph's sentiments and knowledge surrounding the selected Kiowa hymns. The process began with my own construction of the text from these original sources; I essentially transcribed the material and pieced together a narrative from which we could work. We met in the summer of 2000 and began the collaborative process of reshaping the text. Because Ralph and I both made changes to the description as it developed, the following discussion is thus eclectically and liberally drawn from the original sources.

1. All hymns on this CD are led by Ralph Kotay. Additionally, all hymn translations are by Ralph Kotay. I should note, however, that in the process of translating some of the selected hymns, Ralph and I cross-referenced translations with the pamphlet by the Summer Institute of Linguistics, *Kawy-dawkhyah: Kiowa Christian Songs.*

   Each hymn translation follows the two main hymn styles discussed in note 5 to Luke Eric Lassiter's chapter, "Indian Churches and Indian Hymns." Here in the context of this narrative, I should note that each line of translation represents a brief pause in the singing of the hymn. With Ralph's consent, my choice of representation in part follows the poetic style of textual translation discussed by ethnographers Dell Hymes (see, e.g., Hymes's *"In Vain I Tried to Tell You"*) and Dennis Tedlock (see, e.g., Tedlock's *The Spoken Word and the Work of Interpretation*).

2. All recordings were by Luke Eric Lassiter in Anadarko, Oklahoma, unless otherwise noted. Singers on this recording include the J. J. Methvin Memorial United Methodist and other church congregations from around the Anadarko area. In the Christian tradition in southwestern Oklahoma, "singings" are church gatherings dedicated almost entirely to singing traditional hymns. In southwestern Oklahoma, such singings will include hymns from many different tribal song traditions.

3. The members of Ralph's hymn classes have been many and varied since Ralph began teaching his hymn class in 1993. At the time of this recording, class participants included (but were not limited to) Anita Blackbear, Christa Mae Bosin, Linda Bruner, Theresa Carter, Carole Chaino, Marion and Leatrice Doyeto, Patricia Goombi, Marjorie Anquoe Haynes, Richard and Diana Kauahquo, Luke Eric Lassiter, Cathy Lonewolf, John Mathews, Maud McDaniels, Robert Pinezaddleby, Horace and Mary Pinezaddleby,

Virgil Quoeton, Tillie Redbird, Stephanie Starr, Clifton Stumblingbear, Richard and Trina Stumblingbear, Raymond and Marjorie Tahbone, Sonny and Phyllis Tartsah, Sally Kerchee Tonips, Bon and Cherie Tsotigh, Danieala Vickers, and Virgil Wolf—some of whom are featured on this selection and on selections 5–7, 8–10, 21–22, and 26.

4. This translation is adapted from "Daw-Kee, Aim Daw-Tsi-Taw [Great Spirit, Now I Pray]," hymn 330, *The United Methodist Hymnal.* Occasionally, Kiowa hymns are also sung from *Kawy-dawkhyah: Kiowa Christian Songs,* a photocopied publication featuring seventy songs. The words are written phonetically in the Kiowa language, and the translations are written in English. As mentioned in note 4 to the chapter "Indian Churches and Indian Hymns" in this book, the publication circulates among many song leaders and congregations throughout the Kiowa community. But because neither notation nor a recording accompanies the booklet, one must turn to song leaders like Ralph to hear how the featured songs should sound. With this in mind, Ralph has used the publication in his hymn classes to record for his students how they should sing these songs. Although the publication is used in instructional contexts like this, very rarely is it used in actual church services as a hymnal is used.

5. *Indians for Indians* is a weekly radio program featuring live singing and announcements of powwows and other American Indian events in southwestern Oklahoma.

6. For other recordings featuring Kiowa hymns sung by Ralph Kotay, refer to Kotay, *Kiowa Hymns Sung by Ralph Kotay* (Indian Sounds, Box 6038, Moore OK 73153). For further discussions about Ralph Kotay and his hymn singing, see Lassiter, *The Power of Kiowa Song,* 139–51; Smyth, *Songs of Indian Territory,* 66–67; and Lee, ed., *Remaining Ourselves,* 57.

AFTERWORD

1. Donna Kotay and Theresa Carter, recorded conversation with Luke Eric Lassiter and Elizabeth Campbell, Anadarko, Oklahoma, 28 December 2000.

2. Lassiter, in particular, has written extensively about this approach. See,

for example, Lassiter, *The Power of Kiowa Song*, 3–14; Lassiter, "From 'Reading over the Shoulders of Natives' to 'Reading alongside Natives,' Literally"; Lassiter, "Authoritative Texts, Collaborative Ethnography, and Native American Studies."

3. Vincent Bointy, telephone conversation with Luke Eric Lassiter, 27 January 2001.

4. Bointy telephone conversation.

5. Milton Noel, telephone conversation with Luke Eric Lassiter, 12 January 2001.

6. Frances Doyebi, telephone conversation with Luke Eric Lassiter, 24 January 2001.

7. Anita Blackbear, telephone conversation with Luke Eric Lassiter, 24 January 2001.

8. See, for example, Berkhofer, *Salvation and the Savage;* Bowden, *American Indians and Christian Missions;* Prucha, *The Great Father* (see especially 1: 485–533, 2:611–30); Treat, *Native and Christian;* and Wunder, ed., *Native American Cultural and Religious Freedoms.*

9. Important exceptions to this trend have emerged in recent years. See, for example, Kan, *Memory Eternal;* Kidwell, *Choctaws and Missionaries;* McNally, *Ojibwa Singers;* Schultz, *The Seminole Baptist Churches of Oklahoma;* Treat, ed., *Native and Christian;* Weaver, *Native American Religious Identity;* and Vecsey, especially *The Paths of Kateri's Kin* and *Where the Two Roads Meet.*

10. Robin Fisher, *Contact and Conflict: Indian-European Relations in British Columbia, 1774–1890,* 2d ed. (Vancouver: University of British Columbia Press, 1992), 125. See also George Tinker, *Missionary Conquest: The Gospel and Native American Cultural Genocide* (Minneapolis: Augsburg Fortress, 1993), the book jacket of which describes missions as "religion in the service of evil." Ward Churchill has characterized Jesuit and Franciscan missions in the New World as nothing more than "deathmills" that operated as part of the "policy-driven escalations of death" (Churchill, *A Little Matter of Genocide: Holocaust and Denial in the Americas, 1492 to the Present* [San Francisco: City Lights Books, 1997], 140–41).

11. Schultz, *The Seminole Baptist Churches,* 3–4.

12. Treat, ed., *Native and Christian,* 9–10.

13. Clifford, *The Predicament of Culture,* 344.

14. McElwain, " 'The Rainbow Will Carry Me,' " 83.

15. Bointy and Spottedhorse recorded conversation.

Selected Bibliography

Adams, David Wallace. "Fundamental Considerations: The Deep Meaning of Native American Schooling, 1880–1900." *Harvard Educational Review* 58 (1988): 1–28.

Babcock, Sidney H. "John Jasper Methvin, 1846–1941." *Chronicles of Oklahoma* 19 (1941): 113–18.

Babcock, Sidney H., and John Young Bryce. *History of Methodism in Oklahoma.* Oklahoma City, 1935.

Barz, Gregory F., and Timothy J. Cooley, eds. *Shadows in the Field: New Perspectives for Fieldwork in Ethnomusicology.* Oxford: Oxford University Press, 1997.

Battey, Thomas C. *The Life and Adventures of a Quaker among the Indians.* 1875. Reprint, with an introduction by Alice Marriott, Norman: University of Oklahoma Press, 1968.

Berkhofer, Robert F., Jr. *Salvation and the Savage: An Analysis of Protestant Missions and American Indian Response, 1787–1862.* New York: Atheneum, 1972.

Bowden, Henry Warner. *American Indians and Christian Missions: Studies in Cultural Conflict.* Chicago: University of Chicago Press, 1981.

Boyd, Maurice. *Kiowa Voices.* 2 vols. Fort Worth: Texas Christian University Press, 1981, 1983.

Buntin, Martha. "History of the Kiowa, Comanche, and Wichita Agency." *Panhandle-Plains Historical Review* 4 (1931): 62–78.

———. "The Quaker Indian Agents of the Kiowa, Comanche, and Wichita Indian Reservation." *Chronicles of Oklahoma* 10 (1932): 204–18.

Burdette, Mary G., ed. *Young Women among Blanket Indians: The Trio at Rainy Mountain.* Chicago: R. R. Donnelley and Sons, 1898.

Clark, Blue. *Lone Wolf v. Hitchcock: Treaty Rights and Indian Law at the End of the Nineteenth Century.* Lincoln: University of Nebraska Press, 1994.

Clifford, James. *The Predicament of Culture: Twentieth-Century Ethnography, Literature, and Art.* Cambridge MA: Harvard University Press, 1988.

Cochrane, Candace P. "Between a Dry Tree and a Green Tree: Using Photographs to Explore Kiowa and Comanche Perspectives of Their History in the Post-Allotment Period, 1887–1945." Ph.D. dissertation, Harvard University, 1995.

Corwin, Hugh. *The Kiowa Indians, Their History and Life Stories.* Lawton OK: By the author, 1958.

———. "Protestant Missionary Work among the Kiowas and Comanches." *Chronicles of Oklahoma* 46 (1968): 41–67.

———. "Saddle Mountain Mission and Church." *Chronicles of Oklahoma* 36 (1958): 118–30.

Crawford, Isabel. *Joyful Journey: Highlights on the High Way: An Autobiography.* Philadelphia: Judson Press, 1951.

———. *Kiowa: A Woman Missionary in Indian Territory.* 1915. Reprint, with an introduction by Clyde Ellis, Lincoln: University of Nebraska Press, 1998.

Cutler, Lee. "Lawrie Tatum and the Kiowa Agency, 1869–1873." *Arizona and the West* 13 (1971): 221–44.

Dane, John Preston. "A History of Baptist Missions among the Plains Indians of Oklahoma." Ph.D. dissertation, Central Baptist Theological Seminary, Kansas City KS, 1955.

"Daw-Kee, Aim Daw-Tsi-Taw [Great Spirit, Now I Pray]." In *United Methodist Hymnal,* hymn 330. Nashville TN: United Methodist Publishing House, 1989.

DeMallie, Raymond J., ed. *The Sixth Grandfather: Black Elk's Teachings Given to John G. Neihardt.* Lincoln: University of Nebraska Press, 1984.

Ellis, Clyde. "Boarding School Life at the Kiowa-Comanche Agency, 1893–1920." *The Historian* 58 (1996): 777–93.

———. "'A Remedy for Barbarism': Indian Schools, the Civilizing Program, and the Kiowa-Comanche-Apache Reservation, 1871–1915." *American Indian Culture and Research Journal* 18 (1994): 85–120.

———. " 'She Gave Us the Jesus Way:' Isabel Crawford, the Kiowas, and the Saddle Mountain Indian Baptist Church." In *Kiowa: A Woman Missionary in Indian Territory,* by Isabel Crawford, v–xxii. 1915. Reprint, with an introduction by Clyde Ellis, Lincoln: University of Nebraska Press, 1998.

———. " 'There Are So Many Things Needed': Establishing the Rainy Mountain Boarding School." *Chronicles of Oklahoma* 72 (1995): 414–39.

———. " 'There Is No Doubt the Dances Should Be Curtailed': Indian Dances and Federal Policy on the Southern Plains, 1880–1930." *Pacific Historical Review* (forthcoming).

———. *To Change Them Forever: Indian Education at the Rainy Mountain Boarding School, 1893–1920.* Norman: University of Oklahoma Press, 1996.

Ewers, John C. *Murals in the Round: Painted Tipis of the Kiowa and Kiowa-Apache.* Washington DC: Smithsonian Institution Press, 1978.

Forbes, Bruce David. "John Jasper Methvin: Methodist 'Missionary to the Western Tribes' (Oklahoma)." In Clyde Milner and Floyd A. O'Neil, eds., *Churchmen and the Western Indians, 1820–1920,* 41–73. Norman: University of Oklahoma Press, 1985.

Foreman, Grant. "Historical Background of the Kiowa-Comanche Reservation." *Chronicles of Oklahoma* 19 (1941): 129–40.

Foster, Morris W. *Being Comanche: A Social History of an American Indian Community.* Tucson: University of Arizona Press, 1991.

Giglio, Virginia. *Southern Cheyenne Women's Songs.* Norman: University of Oklahoma Press, 1994.

Hagan, William T. "Adjusting to the Opening of the Kiowa, Comanche, and Kiowa-Apache Reservation." In Peter Iverson, ed., *The Plains Indians of the Twentieth Century,* 11–30. Norman: University of Oklahoma Press, 1985.

———. "Kiowas, Comanches, and Cattlemen, 1867–1906: A Case Study of the Failure of U.S. Reservation Policy." *Pacific Historical Review* 40 (1971): 333–55.

———. "The Reservation Policy: Too Little and Too Late." In Jane F. Smith and Robert M. Kvasnicka, eds., *Indian-White Relations: A Persistent Paradox,* 157–69. Washington DC: Howard University Press, 1976.

———. *United States-Comanche Relations: The Reservation Years.* Norman: University of Oklahoma Press, 1990.

Hayne, Coe. *Kiowa Turning.* New York: Council on Finance and Promotion of the Northern Baptist Convention, 1944.

The Heroine of Saddle Mountain. Chicago: Women's American Baptist Home Mission Society, 1917.

Herring, Rebecca. "Failed Assimilation: Anglo Women on the Kiowa-Comanche Reservation, 1867–1906." M.A. thesis, Texas Tech University, 1983.

———. "Their Work Was Never Done: Women Missionaries on the Kiowa-Comanche Reservation." *Chronicles of Oklahoma* 64 (1986): 68–82.

Horse, Billy Evans, and Luke E. Lassiter. "A Tribal Chair's Perspective on Inherent Sovereignty." *St. Thomas Law Review* 10 (1997): 79–86.

Hume, C. Ross. "Notes of Missions and Missionaries among the Kiowa, Comanche, and Wichita Indians." *Chronicles of Oklahoma* 29 (1951): 113–16.

Hymes, Dell. *"In Vain I Tried to Tell You": Essays in Native American Ethnopoetics.* Philadelphia: University of Pennsylvania Press, 1981.

John, Elizabeth A. H. "An Earlier Chapter of Kiowa History." *New Mexico Historical Review* 60 (1985): 379–97.

Jones, Douglas. *The Treaty of Medicine Lodge: The Story of the Great Treaty Council as Told By Eyewitnesses.* Norman: University of Oklahoma Press, 1966.

Kan, Sergei. *Memory Eternal: Tlingit Culture and Russian Orthodox Christianity through Two Centuries.* Seattle: University of Washington Press, 1999.

Kavanagh, Thomas W. *Comanche Political History: An Ethnohistorical Perspective, 1706–1875.* Lincoln: University of Nebraska Press, 1996.

Keller, Robert H., Jr. *American Protestantism and United States Indian Policy, 1869–82.* Lincoln: University of Nebraska Press, 1983.

Kidwell, Clara Sue. *Choctaws and Missionaries in Mississippi, 1818–1918.* Norman: University of Oklahoma Press, 1995.

Kotay, Ralph. *Kiowa Hymns Sung by Ralph Kotay.* 4 cassettes. Moore OK: Indian Sounds, 1981.

Kracht, Benjamin R. "The Kiowa Ghost Dance, 1894–1916: An Unheralded Revitalization Movement." *Ethnohistory* 39 (1992): 452–77.

———. "Kiowa Religion: An Ethnohistorical Analysis of Ritual Symbolism, 1832–1897." Ph.D. dissertation, Southern Methodist University, 1989.

———. "Kiowa Religion in Historical Perspective." *American Indian Quarterly* 21 (1997): 15–33.

Kroeker, Marvin. *Comanches and Mennonites on the Oklahoma Plains: A. J. and Magdalena Becker and the Post Oak Mission.* Hillsboro KS: Kindred Productions, 1997.

Lassiter, Luke Eric. "Authoritative Texts, Collaborative Ethnography, and Native American Studies." *American Indian Quarterly* 24 (2000): 601–14.

———. " 'From Here On, I Will Be Praying to You': Indian Churches, Kiowa Hymns, and Native American Christianity in Southwestern Oklahoma." *Ethnomusicology* 45 (2001): 338–52.

———. "From 'Reading over the Shoulders of Natives' to 'Reading alongside Natives,' Literally: Toward a Collaborative and Reciprocal Ethnography." *Journal of Anthropological Research* 57 (2001): 137–49.

———. *The Power of Kiowa Song: A Collaborative Ethnography.* Tucson: University of Arizona Press, 1998.

Lee, Dayna Bowker, ed. *Remaining Ourselves: Music and Tribal Memory.* Oklahoma City: State Arts Council of Oklahoma, 1995.

Lehman, Leola. "Father Isidore Ricklin and the Kiowas." *Real West* 11 (1968): 34–36.

Levy, Jerrold E. "After Custer: Kiowa Political and Social Organization from the Reservation Period to the Present." Ph.D. dissertation, University of Chicago, 1959.

Marriott, Alice. *Kiowa Years: A Study in Culture Impact.* New York: Macmillan, 1968.

———. *Saynday's People.* Lincoln: University of Nebraska Press, 1963.

———. *The Ten Grandmothers.* Norman: University of Oklahoma Press, 1945.

Mayhall, Mildred P. *The Kiowas.* Norman: University of Oklahoma Press, 1962.

McBeth, Sally J. *Ethnic Identity and the Boarding School Experience of West-Central Oklahoma American Indians.* Washington DC: University Press of America, 1983.

———. "Indian Boarding Schools and Ethnic Identity: An Example from the Southern Plains Tribes of Oklahoma." *Plains Anthropologist* 28 (1983): 119–28.

McElwain, Thomas. " 'The Rainbow Will Carry Me': The Language of Seneca Iroquois Christianity as Reflected in Hymns." In Christopher Vecsey, ed., *Religion in Native North America,* 83–103. Moscow: University of Idaho Press, 1990.

McKenzie, Parker. *Popular Account of the Kiowa Indian Language.* Santa Fe NM: School of American Research, 1948.

McNally, Michael D. *Ojibwa Singers: Hymns, Grief, and Native Culture in Motion.* Oxford: Oxford University Press, 2000.

Meadows, William C. *Kiowa, Apache, and Comanche Military Societies: Enduring Veterans, 1800 to the Present.* Austin: University of Texas Press, 1998.

Methvin, John Jasper. *Andele, or, The Mexican-Kiowa Captive: A Story of Real Life among the Indians.* Louisville KY: Pentecostal Herald Press, 1899.

———. *In the Limelight, or, A History of Anadarko and Vicinity.* Anadarko OK: By the author, 1925.

———. "Reminiscences of Life among the Indians." *Chronicles of Oklahoma* 5 (1927): 166–79.

Milner, Clyde. *With Good Intentions: Quaker Work among the Pawnees, Otos, and Omahas in the 1870s.* Lincoln: University of Nebraska Press, 1982.

Mishkin, Bernard. *Rank and Warfare among the Plains Indians.* New York: J. J. Augustin, 1940.

Momaday, N. Scott. *The Names: A Memoir.* Tucson: University of Arizona Press, 1976.

———. *The Way to Rainy Mountain.* New York: Ballantine Books, 1969.

Monahan, Forrest. "The Kiowa-Comanche Reservation in the 1890s." *Chronicles of Oklahoma* 45 (1968): 451–63.

———. "Trade Goods on the Prairie: The Kiowa Tribe and White Trade Goods, 1794–1875." Ph.D. dissertation, University of Oklahoma, 1965.

Mooney, James. *Calendar History of the Kiowa Indians.* Seventeenth Annual Report of the Bureau of American Ethnology, pt. 1. Washington DC: Government Printing Office, 1898.

Morrison, Tully. "Isabel Crawford: Missionary to the Kiowa Indians." *Chronicles of Oklahoma* 40 (1962): 76–78.

Moses, L. G. *The Indian Man: A Biography of James Mooney.* Urbana: University of Illinois Press, 1984.

————. "James Mooney and the Peyote Controversy." *Chronicles of Oklahoma* 56 (1978): 127–44.

Noyes, Stanley. *Los Comanches: The Horse People, 1751–1845.* Albuquerque: University of New Mexico Press, 1993.

Nye, Colonel W. S. *Bad Medicine and Good: Tales of the Kiowas.* Norman: University of Oklahoma Press, 1962.

————. *Carbine and Lance: The Story of Old Fort Sill.* 1937. Reprint, Norman: University of Oklahoma Press, 1969.

Paddlety, David L. *Conversational Kiowa.* Chickasha: University of Science & Arts of Oklahoma, 1998.

Parsons, Elsie Clews. *Kiowa Tales.* New York: American Folk-Lore Society, 1929.

Pennington, William D. "Government Policies and Farming on the Kiowa-Comanche Reservation, 1869–1901." Ph.D. dissertation, University of Oklahoma, 1972.

Prucha, Francis Paul. *American Indian Policy in Crisis: Christian Reformers and the Indian, 1865–1900.* Norman: University of Oklahoma Press, 1976.

————. *The Great Father: The United States Government and the American Indians.* 2 vols. Lincoln: University of Nebraska Press, 1984.

————. *The Indians in American Society: From the Revolutionary War to the Present.* Berkeley: University of California Press, 1985.

Prucha, Francis Paul, ed. *Documents of United States Indian Policy.* 2d ed., expanded. Lincoln: University of Nebraska Press, 1990.

Rand, Jacki T. 1998. "Negotiating the 'New Country': The Cultural Politics of Exchange in the Kiowa, Comanche, and Apache Reservation and Allotment Periods, 1867–1910." Ph.D. dissertation, University of Oklahoma, 1998.

Richardson, Jane. *Law and Status among the Kiowa Indians.* New York: J. J. Augustin, 1940.

Schröder, Ingo W. "From Parkman to Postcolonial Theory: What's Next in the Ethnohistory of Missions?" *Ethnohistory* 46 (1999): 809–15.

Schultz, Jack M. *The Seminole Baptist Churches of Oklahoma: Maintaining a Traditional Community.* Norman: University of Oklahoma Press, 1999.

Smyth, Willie. *Songs of Indian Territory: Native American Music Traditions of Oklahoma.* Oklahoma City: Center for the American Indian, 1989.

Steele, Aubrey. "The Beginning of Quaker Administration of Indian Affairs in Oklahoma." *Chronicles of Oklahoma* 17 (1939): 364–92.

———. "Lawrie Tatum's Indian Policy." *Chronicles of Oklahoma* 22 (1944): 83–98.

———. "Quaker Control of the Kiowa-Comanche Agency." M.A. thesis, University of Oklahoma, 1938.

Stewart, Martha. "The Indian Mission Conference of Oklahoma." *Chronicles of Oklahoma* 40 (1962–63): 330–36.

Summer Institute of Linguistics. *Kawy-dawkhyah: Kiowa Christian Songs.* Santa Ana CA: Wycliffe Bible Translators, 1962.

Tatum, Lawrie. *Our Red Brothers and the Peace Policy of President U. S. Grant.* 1899. Reprint, with a foreword by Richard Ellis, Lincoln: University of Nebraska Press, 1970.

Tedlock, Dennis. *The Spoken Word and the Work of Interpretation.* Philadelphia: University of Pennsylvania Press, 1983.

Treat, James, ed. *Native and Christian: Indigenous Voices on Religious Identity in the United States and Canada.* New York: Routledge, 1996.

Unrau, William E. "Investigation or Probity? Investigations into the Affairs of the Kiowa-Comanche Agency, 1867." *Chronicles of Oklahoma* 42 (1964): 300–19.

Vecsey, Christopher. *On the Padres' Trail.* Notre Dame IN: University of Notre Dame Press, 1996.

———. *The Paths of Kateri's Kin.* Notre Dame IN: University of Notre Dame Press, 1997.

———. *Where the Two Roads Meet.* Notre Dame IN: University of Notre Dame Press, 1999.

Vernon, Walter. "Methodist Beginnings among Southwest Oklahoma Indians." *Chronicles of Oklahoma* 58 (1980–81): 392–411.

Wallace, Ernest, and E. Adamson Hoebel. *The Comanches: Lords of the Southern Plains.* Norman: University of Oklahoma Press, 1952.

Weaver, Jace, ed. *Native American Religious Identity: Unforgotten Gods.* Maryknoll NY: Orbis Books, 1998.

White, E. E. *Experiences of a Special Indian Agent.* 1893. Reprint, with an introduction by Edward Everett Dale, Norman: University of Oklahoma Press, 1965.

Wild, George Posey. "History of Education of Plains Indians of Southwest Oklahoma since the Civil War." Ph.D. dissertation, University of Oklahoma, 1941.

Wunder, John R., ed. *Native American Cultural and Religious Freedoms.* New York: Garland, 1999.

Zwink, Timothy. "On the White Man's Road: Lawrie Tatum and the Formative Years of the Kiowa Agency." *Chronicles of Oklahoma* 56 (1978–79): 431–41.

Index

Page references for illustrations are italicized.